REMEMBERING THE GOLDEN JET

REMEMBERING THE GOLDEN JET

A Celebration of Bobby Hull

CRAIG MacINNIS, EDITOR

A PETER GODDARD BOOK

Published in 2001 by
Stoddart Publishing Co. Limited
895 Don Mills Road, 400–2 Park Centre, Toronto, Canada M3C 1W3
PMB 128, 4500 Witmer Estates, Niagara Falls, New York 14305-1386

www.stoddartpub.com

To order Stoddart books please contact General Distribution Services
In Canada Tel. (416) 213-1919   Fax (416) 213-1917
Email cservice@genpub.com
In the United States Toll-free tel. 1-800-805-1083 Toll-free fax 1-800-481-6207
Email gdsinc@genpub.com

10 9 8 7 6 5 4 3 2 1

National Library of Canada Cataloguing in Publication Data
Remembering the Golden Jet: a celebration of Bobby Hull
"A Peter Goddard book."
ISBN 0-7737-3311-6
          1. Hull, Bobby, 1939– I. MacInnis, Craig
GV848.5.H8R44 2001   796.962'092   C2001-901992-0

Publisher Cataloguing in Publication Data (U.S.)
Remembering the golden jet: a celebration of Bobby Hull / edited by Craig MacInnis. — 1st ed.
[128] p. : col. ill. ; cm.
ISBN 0-7737-3311-6
1. Hull, Bobby, 1939– . 2. Hockey — Biography . I. MacInnis, Craig. II. Title.
796.9/62/092 B 92 21   CIP   GV848.5.H6M33 2001

Every effort has been made to secure permissions to reprint material reproduced in this book. The editor and publisher will gladly receive information that will enable them to rectify in subsequent editions of this book any inadvertent errors or omissions.

ART DIRECTION AND DESIGN: BILL DOUGLAS AT THE BANG

Page 118 constitutes a continuation of this copyright page.

We acknowledge for their financial support of our publishing program the Canada Council, the Ontario Arts Council, and the Government of Canada through the Book Publishing Industry Development Program (BPIDP).

Printed and bound in Canada

Contents

*Turning on the jets: Hull eludes
Montreal's Dave Balon, left,
and Jacques Laperriere.*

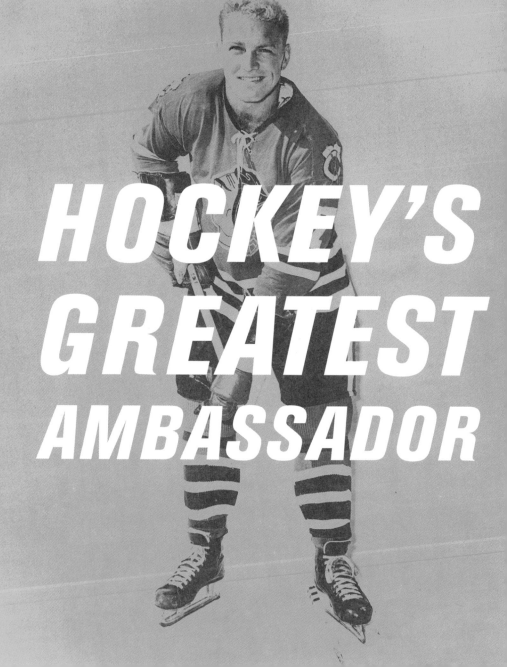

HOCKEY'S GREATEST AMBASSADOR

RECONSIDERING THE GOLDEN JET
by Craig MacInnis

Bobby Hull never tried very hard to conceal the frequent turbulence in his off-ice life.

"My wife made me a millionaire. When I met her, I had three million," he quipped about his stormy marriage to ex-wife Joanne, who divorced him on grounds of physical and mental cruelty and adultery. In his counter-petition, Hull also sued for mental cruelty, claiming her spending led to escalating verbal warfare.

As Montreal *Gazette* writer Michael Farber noted in a lengthy 1980 procedural on the Hulls' matrimonial flameout, "There is no doubt their 20-year marriage was a disaster."

William Wirtz, president of the Chicago Black Hawks, remembered then–Hawks coach Billy Reay saying "that he had never seen anybody fight with his wife all the way down to the locker room and then go out and play hockey like everything was forgotten."

Wirtz added, "Reay often said Bobby would have scored 100 goals if not for the off-ice stuff."

Hull's non–hockey-playing persona was again under the microscope in 1998 when inflammatory comments were attributed to Hull during an interview the retired star gave to the *Moscow Times*. Hull vehemently denied the remarks and threatened legal action, yet the PR damage was done. For hockey fans, who can be unforgiving of their heroes' flaws, the Russian episode — whatever was really said — seemed to reveal one more stain on an already tarnished legend.

It's the usual thing: Once a former great appears to cross the line from heroism into villainy, it is hard, if not impossible, to set things straight.

Case in point: When it was announced, in the summer of 2000, that Hull had agreed to a phone auction of 27 items of memorabilia from his career (including the puck from his first regular-season goal, scored against Boston's Don Simmons on October 22, 1957), the *Chicago Tribune* registered its dismay in a piece reprinted in Canada's *National Post*. Hull's bid to make money from the sale of his cherished game relics was considered the cold act of a mercenary, made worse by its timing — the Hawks were readying for their 75th anniversary season and the unveiling of a Black Hawk commemorative statue outside the United Center.

"Much secrecy surrounds this statue, but it's practically a break-away tip-in that Hull will be featured in some form," K.C. Johnson wrote in the *Trib*. "Much like the Michael Jordan statue, fans surely will pose for pictures next to it, creating memories that will remain unvarnished, free from the desire for profit and money."

Yet Hull only did what other stars have done. Two other members of the NHL's 50-goal fraternity, Bernie "Boom-Boom" Geoffrion and Guy Lafleur, recently announced similar plans to sell off keep-sakes. So why has the Golden Jet been held to a higher standard?

Bedside manner: Bobby makes a young fan's day.

IT'S THE USUAL THING: ONCE A FOR-
MER GREAT APPEARS TO CROSS THE
LINE FROM HEROISM INTO VILLAINY,
IT IS HARD, IF NOT IMPOSSIBLE, TO
SET THINGS STRAIGHT.

"THE BEST PUBLIC RELATIONS MAN THE NHL EVER HAD," A TIRELESS AUTOGRAPHER WHO SPENT HOURS SIGNING PROGRAMS AND STICKS BEFORE AND AFTER EACH GAME. NOT UNTIL WAYNE GRETZKY BLAZED A FRESH MARKETING TRAIL WITH THE LOS ANGELES KINGS THREE DECADES LATER WOULD A SINGLE PLAYER HAVE SUCH AN IMPACT ON THE WAY THE GAME WAS REGARDED IN THE UNITED STATES.

More to the point, why has he never been given full credit for his role in revolutionizing the modern game? Or for his single-handed efforts in not once but twice changing the socioeconomic landscape of hockey and extending its reach into new territories?

As Hall of Fame hockey writer Frank Orr notes in one of the essays in this book, the 18-year-old Hull broke into the NHL with Chicago in the 1957–58 season when the league's stateside image was in urgent need of an upgrade. The moribund Hawks franchise had not made the playoffs since the 1952–53 season, and marketable stars south of the border were scarce. Orr writes that Hull was precisely what the game needed — a dynamic blond Adonis who lent instant televisual appeal to a game that had been neglected by the infant TV industry.

If Gordie Howe's cerebral style was the domain of purists and old-time fans, then surely Hull's cyclonic rushes — and devastating slapshot off the wing — were the dazzling lures that drew fresh converts to the sport. The 1965–66 season, when Hull completed his quest to break the 50-goal plateau with 54 goals and 97 points, was recently listed in a special edition of *The Hockey News* as the twenty-second most important season in the game's history (which, if anything, is a gross depreciation of its impact).

Frank Orr, who covered Hull's record-setting campaign, writes that in the 1960s Hull was hockey's version of Mickey Mantle, Arnold Palmer, Bill Russell, and Joe Namath — a camera-friendly symbol for the game itself. Wirtz called him "the best public relations man the NHL ever had," a tireless autographer who spent hours signing

Hullabaloo: Bobby signs autographs at Toronto's Canadian National Exibition.

programs and sticks before and after each game. Not until Wayne Gretzky blazed a fresh marketing trail with the Los Angeles Kings three decades later would a player have such an impact on the way the game was regarded in the United States.

Hull's second landmark achievement was his decision to spurn the Hawks' contract offers and sign in 1972 with the Winnipeg Jets of the rival World Hockey Association, raising the benchmark for player salaries in both leagues and opening the game up to new markets.

Hull's influence was also felt, quite literally, at street level. In the '60s and early '70s, nearly every kid in Canada played road hockey. After-school games amounted to unabashed homages to Hull's famous "banana blade," as boys borrowed their moms' kettles to steam pliable curves into their brittle Mastercraft sticks. Doug Herod, a master storyteller and former road hockey enthusiast, writes about his "warped" upbringing as an 11-year-old trying to mimic's Hull's style.

In the past 45 years, the Hull name has become something of a brand signature, crossing two generations and conjuring an instant sense of on-ice excellence. Along with Bobby, there was his younger brother and teammate, Dennis, who some felt had a harder slapshot than the Golden Jet. Since the mid-1980s, Bobby's son Brett has torn up the league. In the 2000–2001 season, during a game in Toronto, the former Dallas Stars sniper broke his old man's NHL record of 610 regular-season goals. It is a widely held view that Brett forms the younger half of one of the greatest father–son duos in team sports, a list that includes Gordie and Mark Howe, Bobby and Barry Bonds, and Ken Griffey Sr. and Jr.

"Who's better or who's best?" Brett mused when asked to rank the greatest father–son tandem by *The Hockey News*. "It's kind of hard to comment without sounding conceited. Just look at the elite company we're among." Noting their mutual penchant for outspokenness, Brett added, "We're the loudest, that's for sure."

Toronto Sun columnist Steve Simmons, who first saw Brett play as a "fat" and "lazy" 12-year-old, and followed him through his early days with the Calgary Flames, offers a compelling portrait of the once-estranged son who has grown closer to his father as the years have passed.

National Post writer Dave Feschuk comes at the Hull story from a different angle, reconstituting an interview he did with Rudy Pilous, Hull's junior coach in St. Catharines and the bench boss who led Hull's Hawks to their only Stanley Cup. Feschuk's interview with Pilous, who by then was living the life of a semi-recluse in St. Catharines, Ontario, took place only weeks before the ex-coach's death in 1994.

Mark Leiren-Young, meanwhile, looks at the Winnipeg years and Hull's impact on the WHA and hockey in general, while the *Toronto Star*'s Rosie DiManno gives us a feisty, gimlet-eyed view of Bobby's role as a money-making phenomenon. An archival piece from the late 1960s, one of three stories in this book by the great Frank Orr, visits Bobby on his working farm in eastern Ontario as Hull hurls hay bales and talks about bull semen. Orr's piece suggests this

The two Bobbys: Clarke and Hull celebrate a goal in the '76 Canada Cup with teammate Gilbert Perrault.

is where Hull was happiest, far from the madding crowds of the NHL, threshing grain and raising his prized herd of bull cattle.

As a native of St. Catharines, where the young Bobby galvanized an entire city during his too-brief junior career, I offer an account of the last game he played there before being spirited away to Chicago, without warning and a full year ahead of schedule.

Say this. From start to finish, Hull demonstrated an unerring knack for being at the center of things, and for seeing the humor in every situation. In 1980, during a short stint with the NHL's Hartford Whalers at the tail end of his career, he was teamed with his long-time adversary, the great Gordie Howe.

"He's good for at least 10 more years," Howe, then 51, said of Hull, who was 41.

"What he means is that misery likes company," Bobby shot back.

Amid the stories and stats and the vintage archival pictures and action shots, our goal in assembling this book has been to recall the essence of a Bobby Hull who may have been forgotten in the more than two decades since his retirement. *Remembering the Golden Jet* is not an apology for, or an investigation into, Hull's life away from the rink. Instead, it is a celebration of his raw power and artistry and his deeply felt influence on the game, and a reminder of his scorching genius with the puck.

What's in a number?
All-Stars Bobby Hull and Gordie Howe.

A JUNIOR STAR LEAVES TOWN
by Craig MacInnis

For a brief shining moment, he was ours. Then he was gone, snatched away by the Chicago Black Hawks, who claimed they needed him more than we did.

Who could argue?

In the annals of St. Catharines' junior hockey history — including two Memorial Cups (1954, 1960) — few games seem as dreamlike as the one played October 1, 1957, as a new season was about to begin.

Though he, and the fans, didn't know it at the time, it would turn out to be Bobby's Last Stand — a night when some of the greatest players ever to lace up skates touched down in the bandbox known as Garden City Arena, dazzled the locals who'd paid their $1.50 admission, then absconded with our best player hidden in their equipment trunk.

The junior St. Catharines Teepees were owned lock, stock, and jockstrap by the Chicago Black Hawks, who, in the 1950s, visited St. Catharines each fall for training camp, made nice with the fans, played a few exhibition games, then hightailed it back to Illinois for the regular season.

Hull, by the fall of 1957, had been with the Teeps for two years, and was expected back for a third. Led by Bobby and a wiry little 16-year-old named Stan Mikita, the team had made it all the way to the Ontario Hockey Association finals the previous spring, bowing out in six games to Eddie Shack's Guelph Biltmores. In a key contest won by St. Catharines, Hull, according to sportswriter Jack Gatecliff of the *St. Catharines Standard*, had tied the score late in the third period "on a backhand shot with two Bilts draped over him," an early sign of his unstoppable brawn.

IT WAS AS A JUNIOR IN ST. CATHARINES THAT HULL LITERALLY GREW INTO A MAN. BETWEEN HIS FIRST AND SECOND SEASONS WITH THE TEEPS, IT WAS REPORTED THAT HE GAINED 25 POUNDS AND A COUPLE OF INCHES OF HEIGHT. GATECLIFF DESCRIBED HIM AS A "HUMAN CANNONBALL."

In that era, the junior game arguably had more colorful stars than its parent league. Eddie Shack, the future clown prince of the Leafs, was an offensive terror for Guelph, finishing second in OHA scoring with 47 goals and 104 points. Right behind him, in third place (52 goals, 88 points), was St. Mike's flashy prospect Frank Mahovlich. Hull, still young, had finished 11th in the 1956–57 scoring race with 33 goals and 61 points. The Teepees roster also included Johnny McKenzie (70 points), Ed Hoekstra (70 points), Matt Ravlich, Wayne Hillman, Chico Maki, and Mikita.

With that kind of lineup, hopes were understandably high for the Memorial Cup to return to St. Catharines in 1957–58. But all that

Teepees traing camp: Junior star Hull gets a physical from team doctor Michael Zaritsky in this time-ravaged photo.

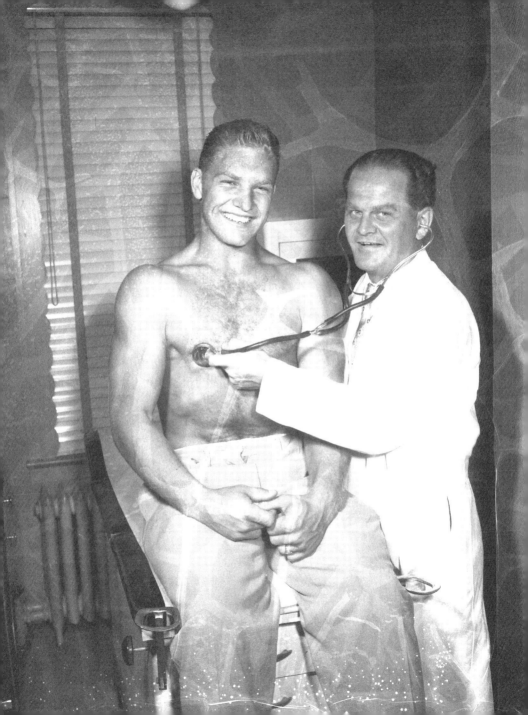

V for victory: Young guns Rino Robazza (left), Matt Ravlich, Stan Mikita, and Hull celebrate a 1957 playoff win.

would end on the night of October 1, when Hull suited up for Chicago in an exhibition game against the New York Rangers.

Hull had spent the morning working out at the arena, had played a high-school football game in the afternoon for his St. Catharines Collegiate Saints, and was back at his boarding house, wolfing down dinner, when he got a call from Chicago scout Bob Wilson, who summoned him to the rink.

"Hanging up the phone, Hull finished his dinner," *Time* magazine recounted years later. "Then, with a full stomach and a full day of sports under his belt, Bobby went out on the ice and slammed in two goals against the Rangers."

The game featured two of the greatest goaltenders to ever guard a crease, Glenn Hall for Chicago, Gump Worsley for New York. The Rangers defense included Bill Gadsby and Harry Howell. Up front was the nifty Camille Henry and the great Andy Bathgate.

The Hawks countered with a defense that included Pierre Pilote and Elmer Vasko. Their top line was the trio of recently acquired Detroit star Ted Lindsay, Eddie Litzenberger, and Eric Nesterenko, but it was the junior fill-in Hull who stole the show.

Teamed for the night with Ed Kachur and Ron Murphy, Hull and his linemates accounted for seven points. His first goal came midway through the first period when he took a relay from Kachur in the corner, worked his way out to the side faceoff circle, and fired. To the delight of the fans, the puck caught the short side between Worsley and the post, putting the Hawks up 3–1.

In the third period, he tallied again. According to Jack Gatecliff, he "traded passes with Murphy and Kachur, then swooped in from his left and pulled Worsley out, flipping a backhand to the far corner. It brought down the house."

Little did the hometown fans realize they were cheering their local star straight out of town.

By the next day, it was clear that Bobby was gone — stolen in the night by Chicago general manager Tommy Ivan. "Don't forget we've been in last place the past four years and we need every bit of help we can possibly get," he said as the Hawks flew off with our golden boy in tow.

In a place where hometown heroes are always meant to move on to bigger places, Hull's departure was still a hard hit to take. "The loss of Hull came as a distinct shock," wrote Gatecliff, who added that "a player moving up too quickly in hockey can be done irreparable harm. Too many times we've seen a promising player hoisted out of junior into professional before his 20th birthday, only to be dispatched to the minors — sometimes permanently."

History, of course, makes jest of Gatecliff's words, but not for those of us from St. Catharines, who never felt sadder than when Bobby Hull was spirited away in the night.

St. Catharines native Craig MacInnis had season tickets for 12 seasons of junior hockey at Garden City Arena.

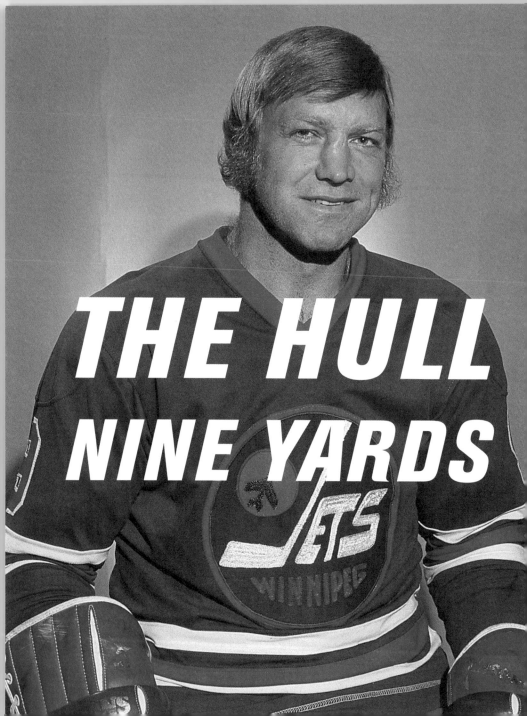

HOW #9 CHANGED THE GAME FOREVER
by Frank Orr

In a Vancouver hotel lobby on the morning of the fourth game in the fabled 1972 Summit Series between the national team of the old Soviet Union and Team Canada with its roster of National Hockey League players, winger Wayne Cashman, the rowdy Boston Bruin who was a member of the Canadian team, handed tickets to the game to Bobby Hull, who was not.

When Hull removed his wallet from his pocket and took bills from it, Cashman held up his hand in the "stop" motion: "Uh-uh, Jet! We all owe you. You're going to make us a lot of money."

Hull, who then shared NHL superstar honors with Bobby Orr, had changed forever the economics of big-league hockey by signing the biggest contract in the game's history to join the Winnipeg Jets of the World Hockey Association, the first modern rival league to the NHL.

By the time the ink dried on a contract that would pay Hull a signing bonus of $1 million and a salary of $250,00 per season, the new league, which had been scoffed at by many NHL owners, was reality. His landmark WHA deal was just part of the large influence the man from the tiny Ontario hamlet of Point Anne exerted on the sport.

Jetting off to Winnipeg:
Bobby joins the WHA.

When Hull cracked the Hawks lineup at 18 in the 1957–58 season, the NHL was badly in need of a major star. The league had such fine players as Gordie Howe, Andy Bathgate, and Terry Sawchuk, who, despite their prowess, were only minor dignitaries on the American jock scene. The Montreal Canadiens had exceptional talent — Jean Beliveau, "Boom-Boom" Geoffrion, Dickie Moore, Doug Harvey, Jacques Plante — but a low profile outside of Canada.

The Black Hawks were about to emerge from a long darkness (out of the playoffs in 11 of the previous 13 seasons) with a core of bright lights including Ed Litzenberger, Eric Nesterenko, defensemen Pierre Pilote and Elmer Vasko, and goalie Glenn Hall, who had come over in a trade with Detroit in the summer of 1957. Stan Mikita, still a junior in St. Catharines, would crack the lineup in 1959–60, adding further shine to the Hawks' galaxy of rising stars.

Hull was precisely what the game needed, the total package that could attract attention for the league and the game, perhaps land a small revenue share in the blossoming U.S. television market (which had ignored hockey), and give the league some impetus to expand beyond its six-city, north-east and midwest base.

By his third season, Hull led the NHL in goals and points and was the league's brightest light, mounting a push for a spot on the list of 1960s stars of U.S. sport — Mickey Mantle, Arnold Palmer, Bill Russell, and Joe Namath.

"The NHL badly needed a star with oomph and appeal to get some attention in the U.S. and Bobby's timing was perfect," said Rudy Pilous, whose path crossed with Hull's several times in their careers.

Pilous coached Hull in junior hockey, was coach of the Black Hawks in the early seasons of Hull's NHL career, and was general manager of the Winnipeg Jets when Hull jumped to the WHA. "There were some super players in the league, but none that really grabbed the fans' interest, and that extraordinary Canadiens club [five consecutive Stanley Cups, 1956–60] was a treat to watch, but they never caused explosions south of the border," said Pilous. "Then Hull arrived with his speed and flair and good looks, the blond hair, the big slapshot, the total package who gave off the feeling that he was a bit of a rascal. There was a void and he filled it full."

THE GAME HULL PLAYED WAS HOCKEY IN ITS PUREST FORM, LITTLE SUBTLETY BUT AWESOME POWER AND SPEED, TOPPED WITH AN INFECTIOUS ZEST FOR THE GAME. AT 5' 10", 195 POUNDS, HE WAS EXTREMELY POWERFUL IN THE LEGS AND UPPER BODY, CAPABLE OF HITTING TOP SPEED IN AN INSTANT, ESPECIALLY MAKING A TURN WITH HIS POWERHOUSE "LEG-OVER" STRIDE.

His favorite move was to gain possession in his own zone and roar down the wing to confront the defenseman in a battle of strength, or a quick shuffle to gain room to deliver the most feared weapon in the game's history, his slapshot.

"When Hull had the puck on your side of center, you could not

Hawk-like gaze: Hull surveys the ice.

blink, because if you did, he might unload a shot and you would never see it," said goaltending immortal Jacques Plante.

Hull played the star role to the hilt. He was gregariously accessible to the media, and not afraid to speak out on what he figured were the game's ills, especially the violence, and restraining tactics inflicted by checking specialists.

His seemingly never-ending contract skirmishes with the Black Hawk owners, the ultra-rich Wirtz family, made for good copy. Hull pushed for what he felt was a deserved salary upgrade because Chicago Stadium was always filled to overflowing. Ownership and management countered with claims they were merely exercising "fiscal responsibility."

Twice he was a holdout in an effort to be the first player with a six-figure contract. He missed training camp in 1968 to get a new deal, and an argument over deferred income kept him out of the first 14 games of the 1969–70 season. By the time Hull rejoined the team, coach Bill Reay had installed a tight-checking defensive system and the Hawks' success allowed Reay to cut down on Hull's free-wheeling attacks.

The team forced him to issue statements blaming his advisors for giving him bad advice and claiming the media had misquoted him. The Hawks did finish first overall, and lost to Boston in the semi-finals. Hull rebounded for a 44-goal season in 1970–71, when Chicago lost to Montreal in the finals, and went on to notch 50 goals in 1971–72, but his days with the Hawks were numbered.

The Golden Jet's sign-all-autographs approach — a signature on every piece of paper during pre-game warmups or as the team's post-game bus was idling — made him enormously popular with the public. However, a few teammates complained that Hull, not the airlines, determined the team's travel schedule.

"We operated on 'Hull standard time' in those days and some guys got a little tired of waiting on the bus until Bobby was ready," said Lou Angotti, a Hawk center. "But, long-haul, he put money in hockey players' pockets, so I guess the delays were worth it."

The WHA knew of Hull's itch for more money in Chicago and his feeling that the Hawks had shortchanged him at the pay window. The WHA's courtship of Hull began when his contract with the Hawks ran out after the 1971–72 season.

Negotiations were conducted quietly in off-the-track places in order to overcome Hull's initial reluctance. Ben Hatskin, owner of the Winnipeg Jets, was an old nightclub operator who understood the value of big-name attractions. Slowly, he won Hull and his wife Joanne over to the idea of uprooting their family and moving to Winnipeg.

Hull's advisor, Chicago accountant Harvey Weinberg, made certain that hints of Hatskin's overtures to his client were heard by the Hawks. But in attempts to land a lucrative, long-term contract from the team, Hull and Weinberg encountered a brick wall. The Hawks would only go as high as the bare six figures — $100,000 per season.

When Hull asked the WHA for a $1-million signing bonus and the newcomers agreed, paying the bonus as a league, the Golden Jet's NHL days were over.

THE HAWKS MADE A LATE OFFER OF $200,000 PER SEASON, BUT HULL HAD ALREADY MADE THE COMMITMENT TO THE WHA. HE WAS THE THIRTY-FOURTH PLAYER SIGNED BY THE NEW LEAGUE.

The Hawks made a late offer of $200,000 per season, but Hull had already made the commitment to the WHA. He was the thirty-fourth player signed by the new league. With some glee, Hull agreed with Hawks owner Bill Wirtz that his defection cost the NHL more than a billion dollars.

"Wirtz told my brother Dennis that my departure had cost them that figure, and when I mentioned it to my accountant, he took out his calculator and figured it out," Hull said. "In increased salaries, all the lawsuits, and decreased attendance in the NHL, the WHA probably cost the NHL more than that billion. I've always felt that the NHL got what it deserved by not treating the players right at contract time."

In Winnipeg, Hull joined center Ulf Nilsson and right winger Anders Hedberg on a dazzling forward line that produced 573 goals and 804 assists for 1,377 points in four seasons plus 82–101–183 totals in 42 playoff games.

Hull was asked how long it took before he realized that the highly skilled Swedes would be ideal linemates. "After our first shift together in training camp, I figured I had added at least a half-dozen productive seasons to my career," Hull said. "They had tremendous offensive skill and could play a strong puck-control game, the style of hockey I liked best."

The Nilsson–Hull–Hedberg line, with the slick, smart Lars-Erik "Shoe" Sjoberg on defense, brought new dimensions to the game. Sjoberg was the first big-league defender to assume a role similar to that of a midfielder in soccer, the "sweeper" who choreographed

Just a blur:
Hull kicks into overdrive.

caption to come

Toro, Toro, Toro!
Hull bursts through the coverage
against Toronto. At left is
Paul Henderson.

much of the attack from the neutral zone.

The big line would rush, usually led by Nilsson or Hedberg, Hull staying a little behind the play to have room to unload his still-big shot, and at some point in the rush, the puck would drop back to Sjoberg, who could deal off to an open man.

Harry Neale, the long-time analyst and commentator for *Hockey Night in Canada*, coached against the Jets with the WHA's Minnesota Fighting Saints and New England Whalers. "That line was the first to use the crossover plays that were more common on the big ice surfaces in Europe," Neale said. "Even the great NHL lines had stuck to their individual lanes, but the Hull line would trade places while the rush was on to find open ice on smaller surfaces. If their space was restricted, they would pass it back to Sjoberg, cross again to confuse the defense, and the 'Shoe' would give to the open man. They were as exciting to watch and tough to defend against as any line I ever saw."

The Jets' approach also made a big impression on Glen Sather, who had hit the management and coaching ranks with the Edmonton Oilers in the late seasons of the WHA.

"THE WAY HULL AND THE SWEDES PLAYED THE GAME WAS THE WAY IT SHOULD BE PLAYED, AND SJOBERG ADDED A NEW DIMENSION TO NORTH AMERICAN HOCKEY," SATHER SAID. "WHEN I SAW THEM, I VOWED TO MYSELF THAT IF I EVER GOT IN CHARGE OF A TEAM, THAT WAS THE STYLE MY TEAM WOULD USE. WHEN THE OILERS WENT TO THE NHL [WITH WAYNE GRETZKY AS ITS TOP STAR], I WAS LUCKY ENOUGH TO LAND THE TALENT AND SPEED TO PLAY THAT TYPE OF GAME."

While Hull's life on the ice was exhilarating, his personal life

Hulluva line: Hull with Jets teammates Anders Hedberg and Ulf Nilsson.

was, well, hectic. A brief teenage marriage in St. Catharines had produced a child, followed by a stormy marriage to Joanne, a figure skater, which produced a daughter and four sons, including future NHL sniper Brett, who referred to his family as "dysfunctional." Bobby and Joanne's relationship dissolved with much acrimony in Winnipeg. Joanne moved to Vancouver, and Bobby would see little of the children over the next several years.

Brett claimed that needling sessions about hockey — Bobby talked of his 303 WHA goals, which Brett countered by saying he had never had a chance to play in the "minors" — brought them closer.

Gazing back on his career, Hull said he would always be disappointed that he did not have the chance to play in the 1972 Summit Series for his country. "Not playing on that '72 team was the worst disappointment of my 23-year career," he said. "I was ready. I was in my prime and I would have loved to have gone at them. The WHA Canadians did play them two years later, but the dew was off the rose. I think I could have helped them in '72 to get in better shape on the ice and in better shape mentally."

Always a critic of how the NHL game was played, especially what he saw as "encouraged violence," Hull feels that he was "blackballed" by the NHL because of the move to the WHA, his role in its seven-season "success," and the resulting cost to the older league. He blames Hawks owner Wirtz, who has remained a strong force on the NHL board of governors.

"I know I could contribute a great deal in management, coaching, or whatever a team wanted me to do, or just working with the league, helping to sell the game," Hull said. "But no one ever has offered me a job and I know why. There are many teams that haven't done much for a long time, and the problem is not enough Sathers who can build a winner.

"The NHL has major problems at all levels. In the 2000–01 season, there were as many as eight teams for sale and no big lineup of buyers. They've taken the game away from the most important people. It used to be a family sport a guy could take his wife and kids to without breaking him, but not now. They'll be losing a whole generation of kids."

According to son Brett, Bobby was never happier than when he was out there on the ice, playing the game he first learned as a tyke on the frozen Bay of Quinte in southeastern Ontario.

"I like, not love, to play hockey, but I could live without it," said Brett, "but my father loved to play hockey more than anything in the world. I can't remember anyone showing more joy at doing something than my dad when he was on a hockey rink."

Veteran sportswriter Frank Orr was inducted into the Hockey Hall of Fame in 1989.

PILOTING
THE GOLDEN JET

PILOUS REMEMBERS HULL'S HAWKS
by Dave Feschuk

Rudy Pilous used to get a kick out of watching his stars boil their hockey sticks. It was a novelty back then, seeing Stan Mikita fashion Bobby Hull's considerable curves by dipping the blade in bubbling water, then accentuating the banana under the dressing room door.

But that door closed swiftly on Pilous. He had coached both Mikita and Hull as juniors; he would coach them to their only Stanley Cup. But two seasons after that 1961 triumph, he was fired by the Chicago Black Hawks, doomed to roam the game's lesser loops for the coming quarter century.

And by the time the Toronto Maple Leafs uprooted their farm club in 1986, Pilous, the director of operations for the St. Catharines Saints, was suddenly out of a job at age 72.

He could not believe that minor-league tickets weren't selling like Michael Jackson albums, that sparse attendance had precipitated both the club's transfer and his exit from the hockey business after more than 50 years of service. He raised his caterpillar eyebrows, shrugged his sloped shoulders, and explained his frustration to the assembled media.

"I tried," he sighed, beginning a farewell address that would

Bench boss: A dapper Pilous watches his Hawks.

become local legend. "But people in this town wouldn't pay five bucks to see Christ ride up on a jackass!"

Eight years later, it was as though that cynical spunk had been drained from his soul. His wife, Margaret, had been rendered a paraplegic after falling out of bed and breaking her neck while answering a late-night phone call. He had suffered a stroke that made walking to the end of his driveway an epic trek. And when he answered a call from a reporter requesting an interview, he declined the company just as he bemoaned his loneliness. He said he didn't like questions, but he also let slip that he loved chocolate bars. So a swap was arranged between a rookie scribe and the last man to coach the Black Hawks to the Cup: Cadbury four-packs in exchange for old stories.

The tape rolled as the hockey man reminisced. He told of his proudest moments first. He remembered the celebration that followed the Black Hawks' 1961 Cup victory, when the players affectionately pelted him with dinner rolls and dropped the hallowed chalice a half-dozen times because, as he recalled, "They were all half stiff." And he remembered the time when, as coach of the St. Catharines Teepees, he pulled his goalie with the faceoff in his team's end, an unheard-of tactical decision that actually spurred a game-tying goal that was a crucial step in the Teepees' march to the 1954 Memorial Cup, emblematic of Canadian junior supremacy.

"It was a good move," he said. "I made a lot of good moves. I made some bad ones, too." From one of those, he did not hide: There was this pimply kid from Brantford whom the World Hockey Association's Winnipeg Jets might have had the chance to land if only

Pilous — the team's general manager in the late 1970s — had considered Wayne Gretzky worth a look. "I thought he was too small and too slow," said Pilous. "But I was wrong."

As a prospector, though, that was his rare oversight. He once wooed a questionable skater named Pierre Pilote to St. Catharines by speaking to Pilote's francophone mother in a fake French accent. And his St. Catharines teams of the 1950s were so stocked with talent, he was given the Black Hawks coaching job in 1957 and promptly turned the Original Six's perennial sixth-placers into championship contenders.

There was glory in working in the big leagues. There was the fun of having Montreal's hockey-crazed merchants banish him from their establishments. "They'd say, 'Shoo, Piloo! Shoo, Piloo!' It was nice to be recognized." And there was the pride of watching his Hall of Fame–bound favorites excel in the pros after he had recruited and tutored them in the junior ranks.

Pilous had known Hull and Mikita since they were teenagers; he got them summer jobs at a factory where their only duties were afternoon naps. And while his prized duo had in common a knack for all things athletic, their approaches were as dissimilar on the ice as they were on the high-school football field, where they both starred.

"Mikita could go around anyone," said Pilous. "Hull would go through everyone." To that end, Pilous recalled how he always had trouble convincing Glenn Hall, the Black Hawks goaltender, to report to training camp on time. "He always said he was painting the barn," said Pilous. "Bullshit. He just didn't like facing Hull's

If **YOU ALWAYS DO** YOUR **BEST** *The WORST* CAN'T HAPPEN
B.C. FORBES

JIMMY JOY

BOB EWER

**PILOUS HAD KNOWN HULL AND MIKIT
THEM SUMMER JOBS AT A FACTORY WHER**

*Pep talk: Rudy delivers a dressing-room
soliloquy in St. Catharines. Hull (far left)
and Mikita (second from right) listen in.*

slapshot every goddamn day."

Hall has confirmed this, citing practices during which the Golden Jet would fire hundred-mile-an-hour boomers from close range while the rest of his teammates lobbed warm-up wrist shots at Mr. Goalie's pads. It got so bad that Hall — who played without a mask but never lost a tooth to a puck — would skate into the corner when it was Hull's turn to shoot. But Hull, instead of targeting the empty net, would zing a hot one into the corner in protest.

Pilous said he devised a way to avoid such confrontations. He often employed a wooden dummy to guard the net during his practices, reasoning that the impediment would make his players think about picking the corners and save his keeper plenty of grief.

"I always tried to make adjustments," he said. And after a long pause (everything he said came after a long pause), he offered his thesis on the modern-day NHL: "There's not enough smartness in the game anymore."

The final interview he ever gave, in the autumn of 1994, is now a murmur on a tape player. He sounds uninterested in most of the questions. He speaks softly and slowly, and his words are hard to discern above the hiss of the wobbly cassette. He laments a dressing room revolt that spurred his demise; he speaks with reverence for the skills of Hull and the others, but with scorn for the way his troops facilitated his release. And then he is asked about that day in 1963, when he opened a letter that informed him he had been fired by the only NHL team he ever coached. His voice rises to an unmistakable growl. He asks how the Hawks are doing this year, but he already knows the answer.

Keep your stick on the ice: Rudy Pilous talks tactics with his young Teepees, including Hull.

"They haven't won a Cup since," he heaves. "And goddammit, I don't think they ever will."

National Post sportswriter and St. Catharines native Dave Feschuk *was the last reporter to interview Rudy Pilous before his death in 1994.*

WARP
SPEED AHEAD

THE SHOT HEARD 'ROUND THE WORLD
by Frank Orr

The Shot was perhaps the most feared weapon in hockey history, often delivered when Bobby Hull was skating flat out. The puck came off the curved blade of a hockey stick that started straight up in the air like a golfer on the tee, except that the "tee" and the swinger were moving at 30 miles per hour, the "hook" in the blade causing the puck to dip, curve, and flutter on its way to the net.

"The shot at 119 miles an hour?" Hull said. "I don't know. Somebody said that but I wonder what they timed it with. It was hard enough to go into the net a few times."

Seven seasons before Hull arrived with the Chicago Black Hawks, Bernie "Boom-Boom" Geoffrion joined the Montreal Canadiens out of junior hockey, where he claimed discovery of the slapshot by accident. As "Boomer" tells the story, he missed the net with a wrist shot during practice and, in a fit of temper, took a golf swing at the puck. When the puck not only went in but through the net, Geoffrion thought, "Eureka!"

Geoffrion continued to slap the puck when he reached the NHL, and when a few of the shots became goals, other players did the same. Before long, the lives of goalies, never a walk in the park, became a

Classic form: Hull unleashes his
deadly slapper.

preview of hell as slapped pucks travelled in their direction faster than ever before. Not only that, but if the slapped puck struck an obstacle — say a player's body or stick — the erratic deflection could also do serious harm.

Hull slowly developed his slapper, an evolution that speeded up considerably when his young Hawk mate, Stan Mikita, regularly used a stick with a curve in the blade, which, he claimed, made the puck easier to control. Mikita also knew it was harder for netminders to predict the puck's trajectory.

Andy Bathgate, the brilliant forward of the New York Rangers, insists to this day that he pioneered the "banana blade" and Mikita copied the approach. No matter who was first, Hull made the best use of the curve, a sharper hook than Mikita's more rounded bend.

"I always thought that the curve made the puck spin when I hit it right, then dip, like the old drop-ball in baseball, before it got to the net," Hull said. "But, again, I couldn't prove it dropped any more than a pitcher could prove his pitch was a drop. I suppose the big thing about either is that if the batter or the goalie figures that the ball or puck goes down, then it's something else for them to be thinking about other than hitting the ball or stopping the puck."

The arc of Hull's stick when delivering the slapper was different than other hard shooters. His stick flattened out well before it contacted the puck, sliding along the ice, and the puck was on his blade longer than any other slapper, a split second or so, before rocketing off towards the net.

"'BOOM-BOOM' SLAPPED THE PUCK HARD, AND SO DID JEAN BELIVEAU AND DOUG MOHNS, TOO, AND A FEW OTHERS DEVELOPED GOOD SLAPPERS," SAID JACQUES PLANTE, THE BRILLIANT CANADIENS GOALIE WHO WAS THE FIRST TO WEAR A FACE-MASK, A MOVE HE ADMITTED WAS INSPIRED BY THE SLAPSHOT, ESPECIALLY THE MISSILES FIRED BY HULL.

"The number of goals increased, but it wasn't because the slapper was beating more goalies. Many times, the slapshot would hit the goalie. But because of the speed of it, more scores came off deflections. When something going that fast changed direction, you had little chance to catch up to it. When Hull came to the NHL and you saw the enormous power in his arms and legs, from the first shift you watched him play, you knew he was going to be a special player."

Dangerous curve: The stick Hull used to score goal number 450.

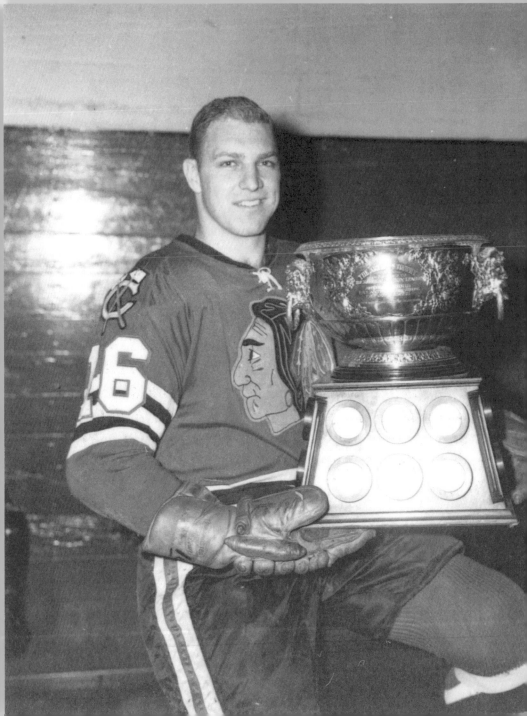

Plante claimed that being hit by a Hull slapper was no fun, even if it prevented a goal.

"Even with a goalie's padding, a Hull shot can really hurt," Plante said. "His shot hit my arm a couple of times and it made the arm go numb. I'd have to go to the bench for an equipment repair until the feeling returned."

Another splendid Canadiens goalie, Ken Dryden, faced Hull in a playoff final and during one regular season before the Jet flew off to the WHA. Dryden did some math to prove Hull's shot was unstoppable when accurate. He claimed that if Hull fired a shot at 120 mph from 60 feet away and it was heading for the top corner, two feet above his glove, it was impossible to stop.

"At that speed, the puck goes from the stick to the net in 0.352 seconds," Dryden said. "In that minute bit of time, my brain can't decide what to do, tell my hand to lift, and have my hand obey the command."

Hull's shot did not inflict any grievous wounds on goalies or defenders, but he did kayo one of the NHL's last maskless goalies, Lorne "Gump" Worsley, who was hit on the face by a Hull drive when Worsley was a Canadien.

"The flat side of the puck hit me," Worsley said. "If it had been the edge of the puck, well, they could have called the undertaker."

Hockey columnist Frank Orr was the Toronto Star's *NHL beat reporter during Hull's hard-shooting heyday.*

51

Big shot: In 1960 Hull poses with the Art Ross Trophy, an award he would win three times.

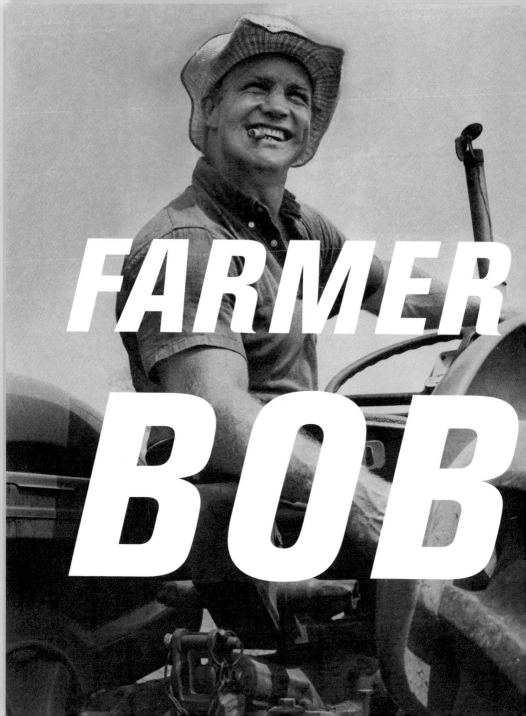

FARMER

BOB

"HAY? HULL HAS IT . . . AND MAKES IT"
by Frank Orr, Toronto Star, July 20, 1968

DEMORESTVILLE, Ont. — Dinner was over. The laird of Hullvue
Farm in Prince Edward County relaxed, as all farmers do, after the
noon meal and chomped on a cigar. (On the farm, dinner is served at
noon, supper in the evening. Lunch is something you eat at 10:30
a.m. and 3 p.m.)

The world's best hockey player, Bobby Hull, wearing work boots
and pants, plus a sports shirt that one flex of all those muscles would
have reduced to a rag for polishing the car, asked his partner, Ralph
Richards, how they should spend the afternoon. Ralph, a chunky
man who smiles almost as much as his farming pal, said they should
haul in the hay, baled that morning.

Robert Marvin Hull, the Golden Jet of the Chicago Black Hawks
who may become the National Hockey League's first $100,000 player
this coming season, thought it was a pretty good idea. He puffed on
his stogie, flashed the smile that has made thousands of doting little
boys and admiring females feel 10 feet tall, and talked about his
farms.

There's little doubt that farming is the real love of Hull's life. Oh,
hockey is fine. It's made everything possible — the fat salary, the

*Down on the farm: Hull at work
on his eastern Ontario spread.*

summer home on Big Island in the Bay of Quinte and a Chicago residence during hockey season, the endorsements for everything from hockey sticks to swimming trunks, and an agricultural empire of almost 1,000 acres and 130 head of prized Polled Hereford beef cattle.

Ask Hull a hockey question on a hot July day. The answer is honest, but brief. Query him about his cattle, he unwinds. He's no gentleman farmer, with a few show cattle, who thinks artificial insemination is a bunch of paper flowers. Hull is a serious farmer, who, along with Richards, a lifelong son of the soil, has built up one of the best Hereford herds in the province.

"Some people think ole Bob is just fooling on the farm to kill time in the summer," Richards said. "That's wrong. When he's here, he works at it. Anyone who doesn't think so should try building a load of 75-pound bales with him throwing them up like they weighed about 10 pounds. Farming's sorta special; you got to have the love of the land in you. Bobby's really got it."

Hull was a town boy, raised in the village of Point Anne. Summers were spent on an uncle's farm, where the agronomy bug hit hard.

"I spent all my time there," Hull said. "I helped with the haying, but I really liked the grain threshings, especially all the food on the table at mealtime. Then my Dad always talked of buying a farm. We must have driven over every inch of road in Ontario, looking at farms. There were 11 kids in my family and we all wanted a farm, but we just never got one.

"Then, after my second season in Chicago, I bought the summer

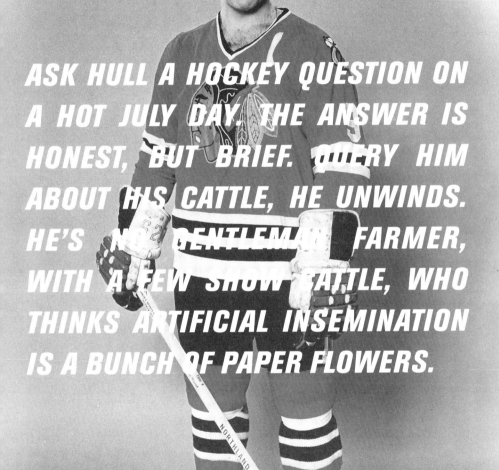

ASK HULL A HOCKEY QUESTION ON A HOT JULY DAY. THE ANSWER IS HONEST, BUT BRIEF. QUERY HIM ABOUT HIS CATTLE, HE UNWINDS. HE'S NOT GENTLEMAN FARMER, WITH A FEW SHOW CATTLE, WHO THINKS ARTIFICIAL INSEMINATION IS A BUNCH OF PAPER FLOWERS.

place on Big Island. I decided to try the cattle business, so I came to see Ralph. He sold me 10 heifers. Later, I bought two farms close to his and Ralph wintered my animals. We've been full partners for the past seven years, although we each have our own land."

They own 650 acres near the Richards homestead, plus another 330 owned by Hull near Picton. Hull plans to sell that acreage to buy more land near the major holdings when it becomes available.

In addition, Bobby, with his brothers Garry and Dennis, a Hawk teammate, own another block of land at Bailieboro, near Peterborough. A feed lot there will hold 280 cattle this winter.

Although Hull could spend his entire off-season making personal appearances, that would mean time away from the land, something he gives grudgingly.

"I have only about four and a half months to spend on the farm each year," he said. "My endorsement contracts are enough, so I turn down a lot of requests. All this is handled by my business manager, Les Stanford, in Toronto. Of course, there are a few appearances I enjoy making. I was up to the retarded children's hospital at Smiths Falls because the kids get a big kick out of it. I also went to Consort, Alberta, a town of about 700. An arsonist burned down their hockey and curling rinks. They had a dinner to raise money for the new ones."

Relaxing time was over. Hull, Richards, and his son Dennis, plus Barry Brownlee, a teenager from Baltimore, Maryland, loaded into the pickup truck for the haying operation. Brownlee, a Hull fan, wanted to spend some time on the farm this summer, flying in from

ROBERT MARVIN HULL, THE GOLDEN JET OF THE CHICAGO BLACK HAWKS WHO MAY BECOME THE NATIONAL HOCKEY LEAGUE'S FIRST $100,000 PLAYER THIS COMING SEASON, THOUGHT IT WAS A PRETTY GOOD IDEA. HE PUFFED ON HIS STOGIE, FLASHED THE SMILE THAT HAS MADE THOUSANDS OF DOTING LITTLE BOYS AND ADMIRING FEMALES FEEL 10 FEET TALL, AND TALKED ABOUT HIS FARMS.

Baltimore. Hull figured he might make an inexpensive hired hand, but after a day, he wasn't so sure.

"Had city kids here before," Hull added. "One didn't last a day, the other left after three. Barry can't drive a tractor, but we'll give him a chance."

On the way to the "other place," Hull stopped to chat with Leland Doxie, a neighbor who was filling a water trough for his cattle. Doxie's son, John, had broken his arm in a fall from a horse that morning.

"Tell him he can have a job driving a tractor for us, if he's able with the cast on," Hull shouted as he drove away.

The second truck stop was at one of the farms, where part of the morning had been spent chasing cattle from a field of baled hay. Richards was left there to fetch a tractor for the haying at yet another farm.

HULL DROVE SLOWLY ALONG THE DUSTY COUNTRY ROAD, THE CIGAR STILL CLENCHED IN HIS TEETH. HE ALTERNATELY WAVED AND HONKED THE HORN AT AN ASSORTMENT OF PEOPLE ALONG THE WAY.

"The cattle business is fascinating," he said. "We have a great herd sire — Hardeen Woodrows Masterpiece. How much is he worth? Oh, I couldn't put a value on him! We have about 300 vials of his semen stored for artificial breeding and we also have some from his

"IT'S ALWAYS TOUGH TO LEAVE THE FARM AND HEAD FOR THE CITY EACH FALL, BUT I FEEL I HAVE THIS GIFT TO PLAY HOCKEY AND I SHOULD USE IT. IT'S ALWAYS EASIER GOING THE OTHER WAY IN THE SPRING."

sire. We'll winter about 300 head. We plan to have another cattle sale August 24. Last year, we had a good sale of about 60 animals."

Hull reached the hayfield ahead of Richards, who was chugging along the sideroad puffing his pipe. Hull didn't wait for the tractor. He pulled the wagon into the field himself to load the bales. His huge biceps bulged the shirtsleeves to the limit and you figured he probably could pull the wagon loaded with hay just as easily.

"I'm in better condition now than I ever am during the hockey season," Hull said, tossing the 75-pound bales onto the wagon with a pitchfork as if they did weigh only 10 pounds. "During the season, there's no way I can do the tough, continuous work I do here in the summer. It gives me a little jump on the other fellows at camp."

How long does it take to prepare for the season?

"About one day of skating," he beamed.

Of course, the talk reached hockey eventually. Yes, Hull thought Jim Pappin (acquired from the Maple Leafs) would help Chicago. Yes, he was sorry to see Pierre Pilote, his teammate of 11 years, go to Toronto.

"The change should help them both," Hull said. "People were getting on Pierre's back in Chicago. They soon forgot all those years when he was the best defenseman in hockey. I hope he has a big year in Toronto."

Mention of the possible $100,000 contract brought an even bigger than usual Hull grin.

"It's a nice thought, isn't it," he said. "I haven't talked contract yet, but we'll get around to it. Right now, hay's the big thing."

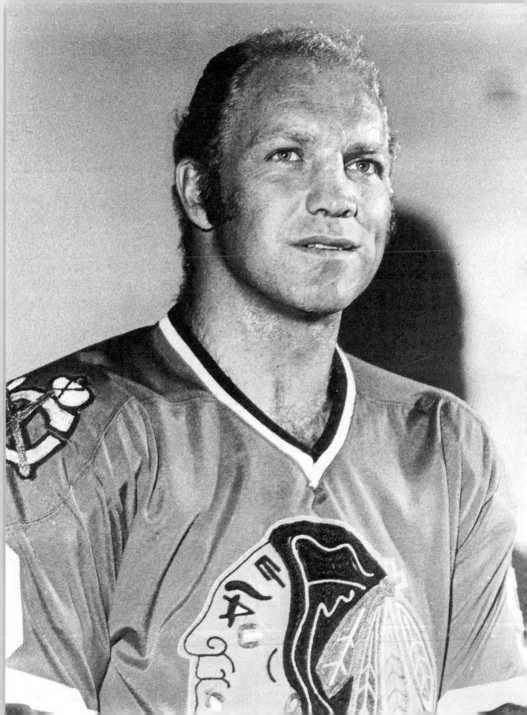

Richards arrived with the tractor. His son Dennis drove it, Ralph built the load, while the Golden Jet heaved up the bales with the same ease as he delivers a slapshot. He and Richards chatter endlessly about the cattle, the farms, and the weather.

"It's always tough to leave the farm and head for the city each fall," Hull said. "But I feel I have this gift to play hockey and I should use it. It's always easier going the other way in the spring. The farm will be a great place to raise my three boys. They love to come over from Big Island, but they're pretty young yet and difficult to watch. There's a lot of machinery around for them to get into."

The last bale on the load was tossed up and hockey's most feared shooter tipped back his summer-weight, white 10-gallon hat to wipe a little perspiration from his brow.

"Drop in for a chat anytime you're in the area," farmer Hull beamed. "A few people stop in every Sunday just to see the farm."

Frank Orr was a hockey reporter for the Toronto Star *when he visited Hull on his farm in 1968.*

BLOND

AMBITION

HULL PUTS HOCKEY'S BEST FACE ON THE TUBE
by Rosie DiManno

Bobby Hull was hockey's first made-for-TV superstar. He was a sports icon, possessing all the visual virtues embraced by a blitzing and glitzing medium that, by the early 1960s, was already well into the process of revolutionizing entertainment and celebrity.

The term "popcult" may not yet have been coined, but as a phenomenon its essence had started to emerge, and television was the medium that brought it into millions of households. Behind closed doors, in the bosom of our homes, TV offered the kind of intimacy that could not be achieved in newspaper reports, nor in frozen photographic images.

It put pictures — faces — to the rush of words that Foster Hewitt had delivered into a radio microphone. Movement, speed, the specific élan of hockey players — at least to Canadian viewers — could now be transmitted, with ever-improving technology, into living rooms across the country.

The faces — oh, the faces. Without helmets and eyeshields, nothing was hidden from view. Scowls, toothless grins, welts, and bloodied noses — all were captured by TV cameras that zoomed and loomed breathtakingly close. But at tight quarters, most hockey players were

65

Matinee idol: Hockey's first made-for-TV superstar.

not things of beauty. As a brutal and often merciless sport, hockey defied all the conventions of matinee idol comeliness. This was no game for the elegant profile of a Joe DiMaggio or the boy-next-door cuteness of Mickey Mantle. Hockey players were made of more ravaged stuff.

But not Bobby. Not the Golden Jet.

He had an open and sunny face. He had, my goodness, *blond tresses* that coiled and curled, that lifted and flew about in the slipstream of his up-ice rushes. The eyes were such a keen shade of icicle blue they transcended the limitations of black-and-white TV. And such charisma. Hull reeked of it, just as he did of virility. Here was manliness, but not dark and brooding, not in the bruised palette more common to hockey players who often seemed so much older than they actually were, as if they wore every year of their lives on their face.

HULL WAS YOUTHFUL AND PHOTOGENIC AND HE ALMOST PERCOLATED WITH TESTOSTERONE. HERE, UNEXPECTEDLY, WAS HOCKEY'S FIRST SEX SYMBOL.

On TV, the likes of Doug McClure and Lee Majors were emerging as small-screen heartthrobs — fair-haired young men who invested their cowboy characters with a hint of libido (or at least as much as TV would allow).

Hull had cowboy sensibilities, too — a cattle ranch was his first and overriding objective. He had the crinkled eyes, as if he'd spent a

Suited to the role: Photogenic Hull was hockey's first sex symbol.

lifetime squinting into the sun. Those muscled biceps, those huge hands, that trademark smile, verging on leer. And heaven knows he had the quick-draw slapshot.

SMALL WONDER MIDDLE-AGED WOMEN SIGHED AND YOUNG GIRLS TAPED HIS PICTURE ON THEIR BEDROOM WALLS. EVEN THOSE WHO COULDN'T CARE LESS ABOUT HOCKEY STARTED WATCHING, FOR HIM.

The irony is that Hull played for the one NHL franchise that did not then — and does not now — allow local broadcasts of its team's games. The Wirtz family, which owns the Chicago Black Hawks, never did understand the potential of mass media, what we call today "vertical integration." Of course, had the Wirtzes grasped the significance of what they had, they would never have allowed Hull to jump to the World Hockey Association, a colossal mistake from which the club has never quite recovered. But it was all about control and paternalism then.

Hull, for so many years acquiescent in his designation as chattel, seeming nothing less than pitifully grateful for his profession, appeared the last person in the world, or at least in the narrow universe of the NHL, who would challenge the system, particularly the reserve clause that ostensibly tied every player to the team that owned his professional rights, in perpetuity if that's how the team wanted it.

But Hull was in many ways not what he seemed. We now know far more about his darker side than we ever wanted to eyeball. Hull would ultimately be exposed by the same celebrity that had brought him riches and fame and public adoration.

In his private life, he was not so golden after all. The man who once staged a one-game strike to protest violence in hockey was alleged to have been a cruel husband, mentally and physically, to his second wife, Joanne, an accusation that surfaced during a very ugly and very public divorce — so much for all those cozy family tableaux in the papers.

THAT KIND OF SCRUTINY WAS THE FLIP SIDE OF CELEBRITY. THE CAMERA NEVER BLINKS AND, WHILE NOT ALLOWED IN THE COURTROOM, THOSE LENSES FOLLOWED HIM RIGHT UP THE COURTROOM STEPS, DAILY. AND THIS WAS AN IGNOMINIOUS HULL IN A DIFFERENT LIGHT, IN A DIFFERENT ARENA, WITH DIFFERENT RULES.

Accused of trying to hide many of his assets from the court, Hull came across as venal and miserly, twisted and greedy. This was the same greed, or so it was characterized at the time, that had lured Hull to the rival WHA, giving that rogue league instant credibility and setting in motion nearly a decade of poaching.

Again the TV cameras tracked Hull's situation, episode by episode. It was manna for the WHA pseudo-mavens, who were delighting in the kind of media coverage they could never buy. The upstart league was cheesy and without great substance, but Hull was the pretty prize — the man in the box. The NHL called him an ingrate and turncoat; the media bow-wowed dutifully. Hull, seemingly secure in his populist image, merely fired up a celebratory cigar and smiled

Grounded Jet: Hull and wife Joanne watch the 1972 Canada–Soviet game in Winnipeg.

THIS IS
OBBY HULL

his millionaire's grin. It was like Farrah Fawcett dumping *Charlie's Angels* the moment her star ascended to its apogee, only to make a string of lousy movies.

Hull paid for his hubris. The NHL took its pound of flesh by blackballing Hull from the 1972 Canada–Soviet hockey summit. Later, the NHL sought an injunction to keep Hull out of the WHA, to no avail. It was a low watermark for the NHL. But neither was his departure from the NHL Hull's finest hour. In fact, because the WHA didn't have a TV contract, the Golden Jet in essence took himself off the very stage that had afforded him fame and fortune. It was Hull's greatest miscalculation.

This is what has to be understood about Bobby Hull: It was always about the money. Making it, losing it, scrambling to get it back. In this context, Hull was both a creation and a profiteer of celebrity and, while the going was good, he milked that celebrity for all it was worth.

More than any other hockey player who'd come before, Hull marketed himself to the masses, tirelessly and perhaps injudiciously. He was the king of endorsements. In 1965, when he made about $60,000, half of those earnings came from outside hockey. There were personal appearances at $500 a pop, royalties that flowed from attaching his signature to various products and services. It was all Hull, all the time.

There were magazine and TV advertisements. He showed off his Adonis body in swimsuits for sportswear companies, peddled hair tonics (until the trademark golden locks thinned to the point where he underwent a hair transplant), recorded a radio show for broadcast on stations across Canada, became an adviser to Simpson's-Sears on athletic equipment, endorsed his own line of hockey gear, associated himself with manufacturers of air conditioners, car mats, cardboard boxes.

None of this was much different from what celebrity athletes do today. But Hull was the first of the breed in hockey, at least the first to promote himself so unabashedly. What he failed to recognize, however, is that all that celebrity hinged on his status as an NHL star, in Chicago and every city where the Hawks played. Without that package, without that TV exposure, Hull's celebrity lost its lustre.

From today's perspective, it seems almost quaint that Hull was publicly reviled for the $1-million signing bonus he received from the Winnipeg Jets in 1972, making him hockey's first millionaire. But for Hull, a lot of money never seemed to be quite enough.

His public image was never the same after that. But, of course, he'd also lost his youthful beauty by then. And with the passing years, his domestic scandals, the unguarded remarks to journalists, his reputation became further eroded, all of it captured for posterity by the media and reported on the supper-hour news. From the moment he left the NHL, Bobby Hull was more gilt than golden.

But brassy, still. Bold as brass.

Rosie DiManno is a columnist for the Toronto Star. *She has covered the NHL since the 1980s.*

A TELEGRAM FROM "BOOM-BOOM"
by Frank Orr

It seemed, for a time, that Bobby Hull would never get his record-breaking goal. It was as if the fates had decreed that no mortal deserved more than 50 markers in a single season. Call it the Rocket Richard Goal Standard.

In a later era, Esposito and Gretzky — even Hull's own son Brett — would soar well past the 50-goal plateau, but those things hadn't happened yet. In the 1960s, a 50-goal season was evidence of genius, of superhuman powers.

The record at the time of 50 in 50, set by Rocket Richard in the 1944–45 season, was probably big-league hockey's most treasured standard. Its merit, however, was much debated. The Rocket had produced his goal-a-game season during the World War II years, when the product was diluted, the teams staffed by many old players and untested young recruits, and the best four opposing goalies in the game were in military uniforms. Richard's record was also achieved with the aid of a rulebook that forced penalized players to serve their full sentences no matter how often the opposition scored with the man advantage.

But nothing could detract from the fact that Richard averaged a

The fifty club: Hull joins the pantheon of scoring legends in this 1962 photo.

goal every game for an entire season. Even when the puck Johnnies came marchin' home and joined the best young players from the wartime league to produce a pro crop that has been called the strongest ever, no shooter could top the 50 mark, even when the schedule stretched to 60, then 70 games.

Richard's second-best term was 45 goals, and the best the great Gordie Howe could manage was 49 scores in 70 matches. But heading into the 1960s, the curved stick and the slapshot had helped to open up the offenses, and the Rocket's record was under siege. When Hull, in his third season with the Black Hawks, led the NHL with 39 goals in 1959–60, he was tagged as the man who would one day rewrite the record books.

But, first, Bernie "Boom-Boom" Geoffrion, who brought the slapshot to the NHL with the Canadiens, and Frank Mahovlich, the moody winger of the Toronto Maple Leafs, had runs at it in the 1960–61 season. Geoffrion made it, counting his 50th goal in game 68, then failed to score in the final two games of the season. When the elegant Mahovlich had 43 goals after 55 games, he seemed certain to top the Rocket's mark, but the pressure and publicity of the chase got to him. The Big M had only five goals in the season's final 14 games, finishing with 48.

Hull's turn came the next season when he scored number 50 in the final game of the schedule at Madison Square Garden, backhanding a rebound from a Reg Fleming shot past Rangers goalie Gump Worsley. Unofficially, Hull beat the record that year when an early-season goal he scored against Detroit, which had deflected in off a

Red Wings stick, was wrongly credited to Ab McDonald. He remained philosophical: "That's just one of the breaks of the game. I had lots of other chances for the 51st goal and I missed them."

Over the next three years, he racked up totals of 31, 43, and 39 goals. The fans in Chicago Stadium, the loudest sports site ever, were waiting for another assault on the record books. In the 1965–66 season, he delivered it.

Hull, who was bothered by a knee injury and a sore hand, scored in streaks in that record season, missing five of the team's 70 games. In 30 of his 65 games, Hull did not score. However, he had two four-goal games, two three-goal games, nine in which he scored twice, plus he scored single goals in 22 matches. His longest "slump" was five goal-less games late in the schedule, when he was stuck at the 53-goal mark. (He would end up with 54.)

Hull had scored his fiftieth of the season in the fifty-seventh game of the Black Hawks schedule, a home-ice win over Detroit. Despite tying his own record, Hull was upset. Earlier in the day, he had decided not to let his five-year-old son, Bobby Jr., attend the game. "I wish he'd been here," Hull volunteered afterwards. "Joanne wanted to bring him, but he's been acting up a lot recently, so I said no."

He added: "Y'know, Joanne always says I take my frustrations out at home — and maybe I do. There are problems. This is a tough life for families."

From there, the press corps began following Hull with a vengeance. Although small by today's standards of pack journalism, the press hordes grew steadily during the early days of March 1966.

Maple Leaf Gardens in Toronto was jumping when Hull arrived to face the Leafs on March 5, a Saturday, with large feature stories in the newspapers and heavy national television coverage. There was also a telegram awaiting him from another "50 Man," "Boom-Boom" Geoffrion: "Good luck. Hope you get it soon. Couldn't happen to a nicer guy."

A piece rushed into print by a Chicago paper listed some of the gifts that fans intended to shower on Hull when he broke the record. They included a Chicago Bears sweater with the number 51 (belonging to Dick Butkus) and "51 models to give the Golden Jet 51 kisses."

But the Hawks did not play their usual free-wheeling offensive game against the Leafs; they appeared tentative. Several Hawks sacrificed chances of their own to feed Hull for his record score. For most of the night, the muscular right side of the Leafs defense, Tim Horton and Bob Baun, kept Hull under control and goalie Bruce Gamble did the rest.

Hull's one big chance came in the third period, when he broke in alone. Gamble was down, the net loomed, gaping wide, and suddenly the puck was under Gamble, no more than six inches from the line.

"I was trying to raise it, but at the last minute somebody knocked my hand and I couldn't," Hull said after the game, which the Leafs won 5–0.

Chicago's offensive futility continued when the Hawks were blanked

1–0 at home by the Montreal Canadiens, then shut out 1–0 at New York.

In New York, Hull almost broke the record on a fluke play early in the first period. Chicago defenseman Elmer Vasko shot from the point and the puck deflected off Hull's shoulder and bounced off the Ranger goal post.

Afterwards, Hull was as relaxed as ever with the army of newsmen, but he did admit to a couple of small worries. His wife Joanne had picked up a heavy cold during her trip to Toronto the previous weekend, and the apple that Hull's mother was keeping as a good luck charm had begun to show signs of decay. "I hope I get that goal soon," Hull quipped. "Mom's apple has about had it."

A Chicago paper's headline asked: "Will Hawks Ever Score Again?"

In Chicago, the drought continued through more than 40 minutes of the next game against the Rangers when Chico Maki finally ended the team's goal famine. The Rangers were still in front, 2–1, nearly six minutes into the third period, when Hull produced the epic goal on a power play.

Hull picked up the puck near the Hawks blueline and drifted through the neutral zone to the Rangers line. His teammate Eric Nesterenko drove hard towards the net, and Hull swung his stick with such force that he almost fell over as he drove the puck past Rangers goalie Cesare Maniago.

"I moved the puck out front for a slapshot," he said afterwards. "I got it out too far and almost topped it, didn't get real good wood on the thing, and it skidded away, skimming the ice. I watched it all the way into the corner of the net, but wasn't sure if it had hit Eric Nesterenko on the way in."

The Hawks would counter twice more for a 4–2 come-from-behind win.

The goalie's perspective? "I saw the puck all the way," said Maniago. "I intended to play the damn thing with my stick, and just at the crucial second, Nesterenko cut across from my left and lifted my stick. I thought for a time the puck had gone in off him. He gave me no chance to make a play."

Maniago shrugged: "I didn't feel as bad [on Hull's tying goal] as when Maki scored the winner. I'm already in the record book for 'Boom-Boom' Geoffrion's 50th goal, so one more won't make any difference. It's those winning goals that give a goaltender nightmares."

The 20,000 fans jammed into Chicago Stadium went crazy when Hull scored. According to one newspaper account, the celebration "was like Times Square on VE Day, a place gone deliriously mad. Hats — enough to stock a store — an umbrella, a model of a golden jet plane, disks bearing number 51, coins, and just plain garbage rained down on the ice as the red light glowed behind the New York goal."

Hull's wife Joanne kissed his hand through the rinkside glass and gave him a tearful smile. And on his way back to the bench, Bobby got another thunderclap of applause when he lifted a hat off the ice and placed it jauntily on his curly blond locks.

Hockey Hall of Fame journalist Frank Orr was one of the reporters who covered Hull's drive for 51 goals in the 1965–66 season.

THE HULL
IN ALL OF US

HULL AND THE ROAD HOCKEY REVOLUTION

by Doug Herod

As a kid, when it came to aping the play of an NHL star in our school-yard road hockey games, my instincts veered toward the primal, a collision between brute power and simplicity that manifested itself in the form of Bobby Hull. The Golden Jet.

Though Hull may have scored the majority of his goals through deflections, rebounds, goal-mouth scrambles, and wrist shots from the slot, in a child's mind they were all the result of rushes started in his own zone, stepping over the opponent's blueline before rearing back to unleash a powerful slapshot that sent the puck hurtling at speeds of more than 100 miles an hour. What determination! What power! What simplicity! The slapshot was enough to turn hordes of youngsters into Bobby Hull wannabes.

Glenn Hall, his own goalie in Chicago, said of Hull, whom he faced all the time in practice: "There are days when you just step aside and leave the door wide open. It's a simple matter of self-preservation."

In game five of the 1967 semi-final playoffs against the Toronto Maple Leafs, Hull unleashed a rising slapper at Terry Sawchuk that practically tore off the goalie's shoulder. It was several minutes before Sawchuk could get to his feet. He stoned the Hawks the rest of the way, a decisive moment in Toronto's improbable run to the Stanley Cup that year. Obviously, Hull should have shot harder.

Hull himself was matter-of-fact about the impact of his shot, which was once clocked at 119.5 miles per hour by fitness consultant Lloyd Percival. "I'm certainly not out to maim anyone, but the goalies take their chances," Hull said.

As if the influence of Hull's legendary shot wasn't pervasive enough on that era's youth, along came the banana blade. The Thomas Edison of this innovation is widely held to be Andy Bathgate, a winger of considerable skill whose on-ice persona was about as exciting as a tube of Brylcreem. The chances that Bathgate's use of a warped blade would launch a populist movement were further dampened by the fact he toiled in relative anonymity with the Rangers, whose somnambulant efforts of the early 1960s put a lie to the assertion that New York was the City That Never Sleeps.

THE TASK OF BRINGING BATHGATE'S INVENTION TO THE ATTENTION OF THE MASSES FELL TO TWO OF THE LEAGUE'S MOST DYNAMIC PERFORMERS, STAN MIKITA AND BOBBY HULL, BOTH OF WHOM SAW THE POTENTIAL ADVANTAGES A WARPED BLADE COULD BRING TO THEIR GAMES.

The new blade seemed to enhance Mikita's already magical puckhandling skills, which were almost impossible for an 11-year-old to mimic with a tennis ball on asphalt.

With Hull, though, the doctored stick came with no special instruction other than to pick it up and let 'er rip. Not only was his

Road hockey heroes: Childhood idols Stan Mikita and Hull with coach Billy Reay.

shot faster than a speeding bullet and more powerful than a locomotive, the propelled puck now leaped, dipped, and curved in midair! This feat was of no consequence to me on skates, since such aerodynamics did not apply to a puck sliding rather meekly along the ice. In road hockey, though, with feet planted firmly on the ground, the new launching device, even in my muscle-challenged hands, would surely wreak havoc. Or so I imagined. For my dreams of emulating the warped-stick blasts of Bobby Hull were just that — figments of my imagination. The chances of me getting a new hockey stick with a curved blade were nil. I was destined forever to be the less-than-proud owner of a succession of straight-bladed Mastercraft sticks, which I suspected were made from Canadian Tire's surplus wooden crates.

The sticks weighed a ton and were stiffer than a Leo Boivin bodycheck, but they also had two elements that were of overwhelming importance to my budget-conscious father — low cost and unbreakability. The other means of possessing a curved blade proved equally futile: Mythology had it that Hull warped his sticks by steaming them. The wood became pliable when heated sufficiently, at which point the blade was bent to the desired curvature. As the seasoned owner of a chemistry set, this steam experiment seemed dead simple.

Alas, I failed. Despite boiling half the water from Lake Ontario

Game ball: The puck substitute of choice for generations of road warriors.

in my mother's kettle, my blades moved not a millimeter. Add unbend-able to the list of the Mastercraft stick's dubious qualities. And so I was left on the sidelines as the youth of my time embraced the new superweapon popularized by Hull and company.

Then, one day, the hockey gods decided to do me a favor. I had an uncle who played industrial league shinny in New Toronto for Campbell Soup, and occasionally the sponsor came through with some extra sticks. My uncle gave me one. It was light as a feather. A fiberglass-wrapped blade. A one-inch warp. Definitely not a Mastercraft.

I RACED DOWN TO OUR BASEMENT, WHERE I BEGAN TO HAMMER A BALL AGAINST THE WALL WITH MY NEW WEAPON. AND WASN'T THAT . . . YES, IT WAS, I SWEAR IT WAS – A DIP, THE BALL DIPPED! JUST LIKE BOBBY HULL'S!

The move to the big time was set for the next day, when my stick and I appeared on the tennis courts of Pine Grove School before an awestruck crowd of classmates.

My fellow grade 8s were suitably impressed. The ball seemed to follow me, my shots seemed so much crisper, even the occasional passes I deigned to deliver were impressive. At some point, I was snapped out of my reverie by a seemingly innocent query.

"Mind if I use your stick?"

It was school tough guy Dale Curtis, a recent transfer from another district. I quickly weighed my options — say no and risk a random beating, or graciously offer up my prized scoring weapon.

After a few seconds, I realized that saying no to an outsider with presumed mob ties simply wasn't an option. I handed him my stick. Actually, I felt good about it in a Bobby-Hull-helps-Howie-Young kind of way. Why hoard my good fortune? Let the whole world in on the wonder of my curved, fiberglass-wrapped blade. Besides, it struck me as something the good-natured Hull would have approved of, too. From my TV room perch, he seemed an engaging sort, always open, chatty, and quick to laugh when being interviewed on *Hockey Night in Canada.*

And, at least according to the media mythmakers of the time, he made time for his fans, signing autographs even if it meant holding up the team bus. "If people think enough of me to want to shake my hand, talk to me, or interview me," said Hull, "then time must be made for it."

So who was I to be a stick snob? Dale plunged into the action, warding off checks, slashing wildly at the ball. After a few minutes of scrambly play, there was a mad scrum along the fence.

Suddenly, as Dale jabbed for the ball in the midst of several booted feet, I heard a sickening crack. Unfortunately, it wasn't the sound of Dale's ankle breaking. It was my stick. My beautiful stick, whose blade was now hanging limply from its shaft.

"Sorry," Dale said as he handed me the mangled piece of lumber.

"But I just got this yesterday," I blubbered, a plaintive entreaty that merely drew a shrug from Dale as he walked away.

The Hull-emulation era was all but over. No kid ever replaced another kid's broken stick. It was strictly lender beware. Unless, of course, you could beat it out of him, an unlikely, nay, an impossible scenario in this instance.

As for pleading with my father to replace the stick or asking my uncle to get me another one — yeah, right. I knew my energies were best directed at trying to hide the fact I had broken this extravagant gift, at least until its expected lifespan was over. I figured on fessing up early the next decade.

The chances of recapturing the confidence I had developed in my slapshot and the general swagger in my game — both courtesy of my Hull-like banana blade — were slim. But hope sprung eternal. Every time the Black Hawks appeared on television, I watched patiently for the camera to focus on a stationary Hull, more specifically the shaft of his stick.

For it was there that one day I hoped to read the word that would instill within me the confidence to carry on — Mastercraft.

Doug Herod, a columnist with the St. Catharines Standard, *still plays road hockey, but never lends his stick.*

THE JET AGE

HULL WOWS THE JET SET

by Mark Leiren-Young

The Winnipeg Jets may not have been named after Bobby Hull, but they could have been.

When the Golden Jet picked up his billboard-sized $1-million cheque in front of 5,000 fans at the intersection of Portage and Main — Winnipeg's windiest corner — any doubts that the World Hockey Association was for real were completely blown away.

This was the biggest single paycheque in sports history. In 1972, basketball's top star, Wilt Chamberlain, was laying up about $250,000 a year and baseball's Hank Aaron was hitting for $200,000.

It was the biggest signing in hockey history — and remains so today.

Yes, it was a major tectonic shift when Wayne Gretzky became a Los Angeles King and set off an earthquake that broke ground for franchises in cities where snow is something you only see on tele-vised Christmas specials, but Hull's deal was the slapshot heard 'round the world.

When a group of businessmen announced that they were forming their own major hockey league with teams in minor-league cities like

Edmonton, Calgary, Miami, and Winnipeg, the NHL brass thought it was a joke. But on June 27, 1972, when one of hockey's hottest stars announced he was joining the Winnipeg Jets, everybody suddenly stopped laughing.

Hull and his legendary slapshot had captured the imagination of media and fans throughout Canada and the U.S. They'd also captured pretty much every NHL trophy and title. By 1972, Hull had won the Art Ross trophy three times and the Hart Trophy twice, as well as the Lester Patrick Trophy, the Lady Byng Trophy, and a Stanley Cup. He was only the third player to score 50 goals in a season and the first to top 50. He'd led the league in goal-scoring seven times and was a 10-time selection to the NHL's First All-Star Team. A January 1970 Associated Press poll named him hockey's "player of the decade."

The league was so unamused by his defection that, as part of the battle against the WHA, NHL president Clarence Campbell told the U.S. Senate that Hull was the property of the Chicago Black Hawks. Meanwhile, the Hawks launched a court action to prevent Hull from playing in the WHA — or even talking about the new league — claiming he was "like an evangelist" who could sway the opinions of players and fans. A Chicago judge actually issued a restraining order preventing Hull from "representing himself as anything other than a Chicago Black Hawk player." Thanks to the courts, Winnipeg's number one Jet missed 14 games before a judge declared the NHL offside.

But the legal battles were a minor-league affair compared to an act of spite that sparked a national crisis, and turned Paul Henderson into a legend. The NHL declared that their most dangerous goal scorer would be banned from facing off against the Russians. No matter what spin the league tried to put on the puck, leaving Hull off Team Canada's roster for the 1972 Summit Series meant the Soviets weren't facing all the best players from Canada. It was an act of hockey hubris that hit Canadian fans harder than a Gordie Howe elbow.

Would Bobby Hull have made a difference for Team Canada? The prime minister thought so. After the decision to revoke Hull's invitation to Team Canada was announced, Pierre Elliott Trudeau sent telegrams to three hockey officials, including the NHL president, urging them to "keep the best interests of Canada in mind" and add Hull to the team. He also told reporters that he hoped the people "responsible for [Team Canada] will be big enough to respond to the clear desire of Canadians" and let Hull play.

Former prime minister John Diefenbaker also took his turn as a hockey commentator, calling the decision to ban Hull "petty" and prophetically warning that keeping the Golden Jet off the team would hurt Canada.

And this was back when everyone was expecting that Team Canada would stomp the Soviet team faster than you can say Tretiak.

While Team Canada skated to the Soviet Union without him, the Golden Jet remained in the spotlight back home. Hull had brought pro hockey to the Prairies as the Winnipeg Jets and the Alberta Oilers (they were considered the province's team for their first season before becoming the pride of Edmonton) prepared to lace up their skates.

When Hull received the new league's first-ever Gary Davidson

Trophy as the most valuable player after a season in which he scored 51 goals and 52 assists despite missing 15 games and doing double duty as a player–coach, the award was almost redundant. By any possible measure, Hull was the league's MVP before he'd ever stepped on the ice. In a nearly perfect end to the season, Hull led his team to the WHA's first championship tournament, though the Jets lost the not-quite-legendary Avco Cup to New England.

A look back at the headlines in the first season shows that no story on the WHA was complete without mentioning how Hull was not only the league's marquee player but also its top salesman. Part of the Hull magic, and the reason he was considered an evangelist, was that throughout his career, he was famous for never refusing to shake a hand or sign an autograph. Kids in all the WHA cities had the chance to meet one of the game's greatest heroes. Hull even criticized other players — in both leagues — who played the game on the ice but didn't promote it when they took off their skates. Hull was even a good Manitoban — he owned a 600-acre farm 30 miles east of Winnipeg even before he joined the Jets.

The Golden Jet was the perfect spokesman for the new league, but what he did best was score goals. In 1970–71, Boston's Phil Esposito topped Hull's record of 58 goals in a season when, with the help of Bobby Orr, he scored 76 goals. But in 1974–75, with the help of Swedish linemates Ulf Nilsson and Anders Hedberg, Hull topped Esposito, scoring 77 goals.

Unfortunately for Hull, since history and record books are written by the winners and the WHA left the arena in 1979, his 77-goal

WHEN HULL RECEIVED THE NEW LEAGUE'S FIRST-EVER GARY DAVIDSON TROPHY AS THE MOST VALUABLE PLAYER AFTER A SEASON IN WHICH HE SCORED 51 GOALS AND 52 ASSISTS DESPITE MISSING 15 GAMES AND DOING DOUBLE DUTY AS A PLAYER-COACH, THE AWARD WAS ALMOST REDUNDANT.

season became an instant asterisk in hockey history, along with the 130 points Wayne Gretzky scored before his Oilers joined the NHL. But forgetting Hull's scoring accomplishments simply because the goals went into WHA nets doesn't seem fair.

A look at the WHA rosters shows the goalies Hull faced were at least as impressive as the puck-stoppers beaten by Esposito in the expansion-era NHL. WHA fans also cite the past and future NHL stars who played in their league. But perhaps the strongest case for the WHA's parity with the NHL, and the most surprising to NHL purists, is the record in head-to-head matches between the two leagues. In 67 exhibition matchups between teams from the two leagues, the WHA won 33, lost 27, and tied 7.

In 1975, in a move that foreshadowed the complaints of many of the NHL's future stars, Hull publicly condemned hockey violence. Since the Jets were the first North American team to rely heavily on European players, they were a popular target for hockey's hitmen, so Hull decided to do something to protect himself and his teammates. In addition to complaining, Hull went on strike to draw attention to the situation. He only skipped one game, saying it was unfair to the fans to continue to sit out, but he'd made even more headlines around North America.

That same year, Hull led his team to the first of four consecutive Avco Cup finals. The Jets won three of them, including the first championship. The only blip in their dynasty was a loss to Quebec in a seven-game series in 1976–77.

A few games into the 1978–79 season, distracted by a bitter and very public divorce, Hull announced his retirement from the game, though he publicly proclaimed his allegiance to the Jets and remained with the team as a vice-president.

The WHA retired the same season Hull did, with the Jets, the Hartford Whalers, the Quebec Nordiques, and the Edmonton Oilers moving to the NHL the following year.

Hull briefly returned to the game, rejoining the NHL Jets for 18 games (scoring 10 points) during their first NHL season, then moving to the Hartford Whalers for nine games (scoring seven points). He also played three games in the 1980 playoffs before hanging up his skates for good.

In 411 regular-season games with the Jets, Hull scored 303 goals and 335 assists. At the end of the 2000–2001 season, Bobby Hull was ranked 10th among all-time NHL goal scorers. But if you add his WHA numbers to his NHL totals, Hull is safely, and perhaps permanently, ensconced in third place, trailing only fellow WHA alumni Gordie Howe and Wayne Gretzky.

Mark Leiren-Young is a West Coast playwright, screenwriter, journalist, and Canucks fan who still remembers cheering for the Vancouver Blazers. He co-wrote the song "Hockey Nut in Canada," which has been played at NHL games in Vancouver and Edmonton and is featured on the Local Anxiety CD Forgive Us, We're Canadian.

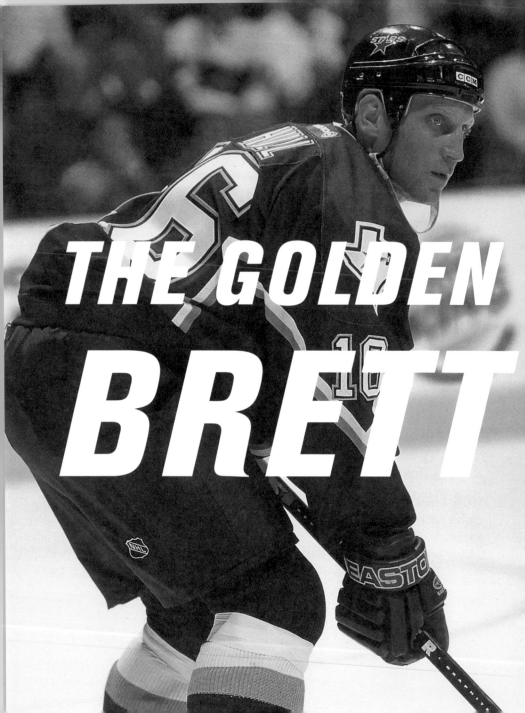

THE GOLDEN
BRETT

LIKE FATHER, LIKE SON? THE STORY OF BOBBY AND BRETT
by Steve Simmons

The scout was sitting up high in the corner of the small arena in northeast Calgary, the way scouts always do, when I looked down at his crumpled notepad.

Two words were written on the pad and then circled, as if to further emphasize their meaning. One word was "fat." The other was "lazy."

"Which one is he?" I asked innocently, pointing to the ice. "Fat or lazy?"

"Both," snarled the scout. "He's the one kid out there who's not doing a damn thing."

That was my introduction to Brett Hull, son of a legend, on a winter's afternoon in 1980. He was playing minor hockey at the time for a team called Vancouver North Shore. "The only reason I'm here is because of his name," the NHL scout complained. "If his name wasn't Hull, I wouldn't be wasting my time watching this."

Brett Hull likes to call himself "the fat kid." He usually laughs in a self-deprecating kind of way when he relates the stories of growing up in hockey as the estranged son of a superstar with a last name that could be either magic or a curse. By his mid-teens, he was well

The next generation: Son Brett, doing the family name proud.

over 200 pounds, and not the flattering, athletic kind of 200 pounds that he is today.

"I can put weight on just by looking at food," he once joked. "It's who I am."

It was three teams and several years after that minor hockey tournament in Calgary that I would meet up with Brett Hull again. By then, he had been drafted by the Calgary Flames, played internationally for the United States, and scored all kinds of goals at the University of Minnesota–Duluth. This was the playoff spring of 1986, and in a small media dining room at what was then called the Olympic Saddledome, with only a handful of reporters even interested in the story, Hull signed his first National Hockey League contract.

The questions, of course, had to be asked. Where is your father? What is your relationship? Why isn't he here? And then the answers came out uncomfortably.

HIS RELATIONSHIP WITH HIS FATHER WAS ALMOST NONEXISTENT, THE RESULT OF A MESSY AND ANGRY DIVORCE. HE LIVED ON ONE SIDE OF THE COUNTRY, HIS FATHER LIVED ON THE OTHER, ON A FARM IN ONTARIO. HIS FATHER, HE SAID, HAD LITTLE TO DO WITH HIS HOCKEY DEVELOPMENT, EVEN LESS TO DO WITH LIFE.

"When did you last speak to him?" someone asked. "He called me last night," said Brett Hull. "He asked if he could be my agent."

For almost half of Brett Hull's first 20 years, his father was

Hull family album: Top image: *Bobby, 12, and father Robert.* Bottom left: *Bobby and brother Dennis.* Bottom right: *Proud mom.*

OVER THE YEARS, AS BOBBY HULL GREW OLDER, AS BRETT HULL
MATURED INTO THE STAR HE HAS SINCE BECOME, THE DISTANCE
BETWEEN THE TWO MEN HAS FADED, THE ANIMOSITIES, AT LEAST FOR
PUBLIC CONSUMPTION, HAVE LESSENED, THE ACCEPTANCE OF TWO TAL-
ENTS OF THE SAME NAME AND LINEAGE HAS GROWN GREATER.

someone he watched on TV. There was almost no relationship after the divorce from Joanne. "I mean, no contact," Brett's mother, Joanne Robinson, told *Saturday Night* magazine. "No Christmas card, no birthday card, no phone calls, nothing."

Over the years, as Bobby Hull grew older, as Brett Hull matured into the star he has since become, the distance between the two men has faded, the animosities, at least for public consumption, have lessened, the acceptance of two talents of the same name and lineage has grown greater. But rarely have two people from the same family playing the same game shared so much success so differently.

"At one time, Brett and his mother and whoever else was advising him didn't want me involved," said Bobby. "Now, he's willing to listen."

Bobby Hull was all flash and dash, with a big smile and a bigger slapshot. He was an ESPN highlight long before there was an ESPN, the hockey player all of us would have been as kids, if we could have closed our eyes and picked just one player to be. I can still see him in his Black Hawks uniform, whooshing down the left wing, cutting to the middle of the ice, the crowd buzzing, raising his stick back with his huge left arm, fear in the goaltender's unmasked face.

Brett wasn't consumed with the Golden Jet mystique, though. He had a father, and then his father was gone. "He was a normal dad," Brett said. "He wasn't much of a teacher when it came to hockey. He was a typical dad. Nothing was good enough . . . . When he did watch me play, which wasn't often, it was never good enough."

There was never a passion within Brett Hull to be a hockey player.

Proud dad: Bobby poses with Brett, winner of the Hart and Lady Byng trophies.

As a kid, he hated skating so much he would beg to be put in goal. He didn't devote hours to improving his game the way his father did, on outdoor rinks, honing his skills, forever playing. "I never had that kind of desire," he said once. "But I couldn't care less if I didn't make it. If I had tried to be Bobby Hull all my life, I'd have grown up old, wondering what happened to my youth."

What he could always do was shoot. Long before he could skate, he could shoot. The same kind of power his father had, but with quicker hands and from the right side instead of the left. As a boy, when his brothers would skate, he would go on the ice with boots on and just shoot pucks.

WHEN HE WAS 10 OR 11, THE STORY GOES, HE SHOT THE PUCK HARDER, QUICKER, AND WITH MORE EFFICIENCY THAN MOST OF HIS FATHER'S TEAMMATES WITH THE WINNIPEG JETS.

"He was a piece of work as a kid, walking around with his fly undone, his jacket open, his shoes sliding off, snot coming out of his nose," Bobby was quoted in the *New York Times Magazine*. "You didn't understand if he was interested in the game. He never showed any enthusiasm."

But, as his father said later, and even the dubious scouts found out, in Bobby's words, "He always did the least work and scored the most goals."

THERE HAS NEVER BEEN FLASH OR DASH IN BRETT HULL'S GAME, AND THAT HAS BEEN HIS STRENGTH AND HIS CLAIM TO INDIVIDUALISM. BOBBY WAS ALL ABOUT IMAGE: SIGNING AUTOGRAPHS, SMILING FOR THE KIDS, PLAYING THE PART OF HERO EVEN AFTER IT WAS REVEALED HE WASN'T NECESSARILY A CHARACTER WORTHY OF ANYTHING OTHER THAN SPORTING ADMIRATION.

Brett has been far more pragmatic, off-the-cuff, and outspoken. His game is difficult to define but remarkably efficient. His voice and his viewpoints are crisp, clear, and unafraid. Image was for the father; honesty was for the son.

Brett Hull gave us a brief glimpse into the future on his first shift in the NHL. It happened in game three of the 1986 Stanley Cup finals between the Calgary Flames and the Montreal Canadiens. Hull took a pass and fired a snapshot in the direction of Montreal's little-known rookie goaltender, Patrick Roy. The puck beat Roy and clanged off the crossbar. It was as if a message was sent out that night: A new shooter was about to arrive.

"The biggest contribution I have made to Brett's success is providing him with the genes to do what he does so well," said Bobby. It just took him a while to do it as well as he wanted to.

There is a common thread to Brett Hull's career other than his sensational scoring and the millions of dollars earned. In each of his three major-league stops, coaches have tried to change him. They have asked him to work harder. They have asked him to be more responsible defensively. They have asked him to broaden his game. They have asked him to play along.

In Calgary, a belief that he couldn't become a well-rounded player led to his being traded away. Cliff Fletcher, who was general manager of the Flames at the time, tells a story of how they finally agreed to trade Hull to St. Louis. Fletcher, in those days, worked as a consensus manager. If the main voices in the organization agreed with something, it got done. Some of the main voices — coach Terry Crisp and assistant general manager Al MacNeil — thought the Flames had to trade Hull if they wanted to make the proper improvements to win the Stanley Cup.

So Fletcher went around the boardroom and asked, "Do you want to trade someone who is going to score 40 goals a year for the next 10 years?" Everyone said yes. Then he upped the ante. "Do you want to trade someone who is going to score 50 goals a year for the next 10 years?" The answer was the same. He kept upping the total; the hockey people never budged.

In one of the most one-sided trades in the history of hockey, the Flames sent Brett Hull and Steve Bozek to St. Louis and all Calgary got back was veteran defenseman Rob Ramage and backup goalie Rick Wamsley. Years later, Fletcher would call it "the worst trade I ever made." Over the next five seasons in St. Louis, Hull would average 65 goals per year, including a mind-altering 86 goals in the 1990–91 season. In Bobby Hull's best year, 16 seasons earlier, he

HIS GAME IS DIFFICULT TO DEFINE BUT REMARK-
ABLY EFFICIENT. HIS VOICE AND HIS VIEWPOINTS
ARE CRISP, CLEAR, AND UNAFRAID. IMAGE WAS
FOR THE FATHER; HONESTY WAS FOR THE SON.

scored 77 goals for the Winnipeg Jets of the WHA. Huge seasons accomplished differently.

Or, in Brett Hull's own words, trying to explain his success, "There comes that moment when I have lost myself and only the play finds me."

Mike Keenan, who coached Hull for two and a half seasons in St. Louis, saw it more simply. There was, in his mind, something understated about Brett Hull's ability to anticipate open ice, to find the right spot, to shoot the puck so succinctly. He had what Keenan called an "uncanny knack." The knack that saw the unlikely son, the fat kid the scouts had no time for, score more NHL goals than his legendary father. The two, who haven't always been close, will forever be united in the Hockey Hall of Fame.

"There are not too many guys — except for maybe Kyle Petty or Michael Andretti — who have followed in their father's Hall of Fame footsteps like I have," said Brett Hull.

There are not too many guys like Brett Hull at all.

Steve Simmons was a sports columnist at the Calgary Herald *during the formative years of Brett Hull's professional career. An award-winning sportswriter for more than 20 years and the author of two books on hockey, Simmons now writes the city column for the* Toronto Sun.

WHAT THEY SAID

Quotable Quotes on Bobby Hull

"NOBODY OF HIS ERA HAS GONE OUT OF HIS WAY AS MUCH OR IS MORE GRACIOUS THAN BOBBY HULL."

– Canadiens goalie Ken Dryden, before the start of the 1976 Canada Cup

"THE FIRST TIME I SAW THAT THING, I SAID A PRAYER OF THANKS THAT I DIDN'T HAVE TO WORRY ABOUT IT."

– Goalie and teammate Glenn Hall on Hull's slapshot

"I'VE PLAYED WITH BOBBY SINCE WE WERE JUNIORS TOGETHER AND THE ONLY THING I DIS-AGREE WITH HIM ON IS THE WAY HE LETS GUYS FOUL HIM. I'D BUST SOMEONE OVER THE HEAD IF THEY DID THAT TO ME. BUT I'M NOT AS NICE A GUY AS BOBBY AND EVERYONE KNOWS IT."

– Stan Mikita on his teammate's pacifist tendencies

"IT HAD TO COME. WHAT CAN YOU SAY EXCEPT TO CONGRATULATE HIM?"

– Rocket Richard, reluctantly, on Hull breaking the 50-goal barrier in 1966

"HE NEVER EVEN HAD TO WORK WITH WEIGHTS."

– Robert Hull, Sr., on his son's natural, bull-wrestling physique

"MY PROBLEM WAS THAT BOBBY WAS SO GOOD. I DIDN'T WANT TO EMBARRASS HIM AND YET I FELT THAT WAS WHAT I WAS DOING EVERY TIME I WENT ON THE ICE."

– Teammate and kid brother Dennis Hull on living in the shadow of the Golden Jet

"HAWKS HAD TRAMPED TO THEIR DRESSING ROOM WITH HEADS BOWED. FROM INSIDE CAME THE SOUND OF CURVED STICKS BEING SMASHED TO SPLINTERS."

– Paul Dulmage, Toronto Telegram, *describing Hull and company's stick-smashing party after Chicago's loss to Toronto in the 1967 playoffs*

"HE'S A STATUE BY PRAXITELES COME ALIVE FROM THE GOLDEN AGE OF GREECE, INCREDIBLY HANDSOME EVEN WITHOUT HIS FRONT TEETH. A MAN WHO INSPIRES SIGHS IN EVERY MAIDEN AND ENVY IN THE BLOOD OF EVERY MAN."

– Society page columnist Tish Baldridge, Chicago Daily News

"WHEN YOU GO AGAINST CHICAGO, YOU'RE DOWN 1–0."

– Leafs coach Punch Imlach, referring to Hull's scoring ability

"HE HASN'T A WEAKNESS. UNLESS YOU STOP HIM IN HIS OWN END OF THE RINK, YOU DON'T HAVE A CHANCE. HE'S TOO BIG AND STRONG."

– Andy Bathgate on Hull's wind-up rushes

"STOPPING ONE OF HULL'S SHOTS ON YOUR PADS IS LIKE BEING SLUGGED WITH A SLEDGEHAMMER."

– Leafs goalie Johnny Bower

"THE KID LOOKS GOOD IN HIS FIRST GAME."

– Gordie Howe, after the 41-year-old Hull joined Howe on the Hartford Whalers

"THE SIGHT OF ROBERT MARVIN HULL . . . LEAN-ING INTO A HOCKEY PUCK IS ONE OF THE TRUE SPECTACLES OF SPORT — LIKE WATCHING MICKEY MANTLE CLEAR THE ROOF, OR WILT CHAMBER-LAIN FLICK IN A BASKET, OR BART STARR THROW THAT BEAUTIFUL BOMB."

– Time, *1968*

"HIS SHOT IS LIKE A PIECE OF LEAD. ONE OF HIS HARD SHOTS WOULD BREAK MY MASK IF IT HIT IT."

– *Canadiens goalie and facemask pioneer Jacques Plante*

"PEOPLE FORGET THAT BOBBY WAS ONE OF THE MOST PHYSICAL PLAYERS IN HOCKEY. HE WOULDN'T BACK AWAY FROM ANYONE AND HE KNEW HOW TO HURT YOU."

– *Canadiens policeman John Ferguson*

BOBBY HULL

REGULAR SEASON NHL, WHA

YEAR	TEAM	GP	G	A	PTS	PIM
1957–58	Chicago Black Hawks	70	13	34	47	62
1958–59	Chicago Black Hawks	70	18	32	50	50
1959–60	Chicago Black Hawks	70	39	42	81	68
1960–61	Chicago Black Hawks	67	31	25	56	43
1961–62	Chicago Black Hawks	70	50	34	84	35
1962–63	Chicago Black Hawks	65	31	31	62	27
1963–64	Chicago Black Hawks	70	43	44	87	50
1964–65	Chicago Black Hawks	61	39	32	71	32
1965–66	Chicago Black Hawks	65	54	43	97	70
1966–67	Chicago Black Hawks	66	52	28	80	52
1967–68	Chicago Black Hawks	71	44	31	75	39
1968–69	Chicago Black Hawks	74	58	49	107	48
1969–70	Chicago Black Hawks	61	38	29	67	8
1970–71	Chicago Black Hawks	78	44	52	96	32
1971–72	Chicago Black Hawks	78	50	43	93	24
1972–73	Winnipeg Jets WHA	63	51	52	103	37
1973–74	Winnipeg Jets WHA	75	53	42	95	38
1974–75	Canada–Soviet Series	8	7	2	9	0
1974–75	Winnipeg Jets WHA	78	77	65	142	41
1975–76	Winnipeg Jets WHA	80	53	70	123	30
1976–77	Canada Cup	7	5	3	8	2
1976–77	Winnipeg Jets WHA	34	21	32	53	14
1977–78	Winnipeg Jets WHA	77	46	71	117	23
1978–79	Winnipeg Jets WHA	4	2	3	05	0
1979–80	Winnipeg Jets NHL	18	4	6	10	0
1979–80	Hartford Whalers NHL	9	2	5	7	0
NHL TOTALS		1063	610	560	1170	640
NHL PLAYOFF TOTALS		119	62	67	129	102
WHA TOTALS		411	303	335	638	183

Career Facts and Highlights

BORN ROBERT MARVIN HULL, JANUARY 3, 1939, IN THE HAMLET OF POINT ANNE, ONTARIO

CHICAGO MOVED HULL FROM HESPELER TO GALT TO WOODSTOCK TO ST. CATHARINES AS A TEENAGER; HE ATTENDED FOUR DIFFERENT HIGH SCHOOLS

PLAYED FOR HIS FUTURE NHL COACH RUDY PILOUS AS A JUNIOR A STAR WITH THE ST. CATHARINES TEEPEES; IN HIS SECOND AND FINAL SEASON (1956–57) LED TEEPEES WITH 33 GOALS

LED CHICAGO TO A STANLEY CUP IN 1961, HIS ONLY CHAMPIONSHIP IN 15 SEASONS WITH THE HAWKS

WON THE ART ROSS TROPHY, EMBLEMATIC OF THE REGULAR-SEASON POINT-SCORING TITLE, THREE TIMES (1960, '62, '66)

ELECTED TO THE NHL FIRST ALL-STAR TEAM 10 TIMES, TWICE TO THE SECOND ALL-STAR TEAM

PARTICIPATED IN 12 NHL ALL-STAR GAMES; APPEARED WITH BROTHER AND TEAMMATE DENNIS HULL IN THREE OF THEM (1969, '71, '72)

ELECTED TO THE WHA FIRST ALL-STAR TEAM THREE TIMES (1973, '74, '75), TWICE TO THE SECOND ALL-STAR TEAM (1976, '78)

WON THE LADY BYNG TROPHY AS MOST GENTLEMANLY PLAYER IN 1965

WON THE HART TROPHY IN 1965 AND '66

WAS THE FIRST PLAYER TO SCORE MORE THAN 50 GOALS IN THE REGULAR SEASON, NOTCHING 54 GOALS IN 1965–66, 52 IN 1966–67, AND 58 IN 1968–69

SCORED 77 GOALS FOR THE JETS IN THE 1974–75 SEASON, SURPASSING PHIL ESPOSITO'S PRO RECORD OF 76

CLOSED OUT HIS CAREER IN 1979–80 DURING A SHORT NHL STINT WITH THE HARTFORD WHALERS, WHERE HE TEAMED WITH GORDIE HOWE

ELECTED TO THE HOCKEY HALL OF FAME IN 1983

IN OCTOBER 2000, BOBBY AND DENNIS HULL WERE BOTH SELECTED TO CHICAGO'S 75TH ANNIVERSARY ALL-STAR ROSTER, AS VOTED BY FANS AND MEDIA

Acknowledgments

I offer a 21-slapshot salute to Jim Gifford at Stoddart for his guidance in helping build the Bobby Hull story arc, and to my long-time collaborator, Bill Douglas, whose clever art direction helped conjure the spirit of the Golden Jet both on and off the ice.

Special thanks to Frank Orr, my former colleague at the *Toronto Star* and a Hall of Fame sportswriter, whose deft journalism, from the late 1950s all the way to the present day, has elevated the genre of hockey writing to an art form.

Other contributors showed a cheerful willingness to work around daily deadlines, including the *Toronto Sun*'s Steve Simmons, who shared his up-close observations of the young Brett Hull, and the *National Post*'s Dave Feschuk, who took time from covering the Toronto Raptors in their maiden playoff series against the New York Knicks to file a poignant piece on Hull's late coach, Rudy Pilous.

Thanks also to Mark Leiren-Young, a certified hockey nut, who took a break from his hectic career in television and theatre writing to offer an appraisal of Hull's WHA years.

Thanks also to the *Toronto Star*'s Rosie DiManno, who was covering an earthquake on the Indian subcontinent when I first began pestering her to wax analytic about Hull, and to *St. Catharines Standard* columnist Doug Herod, who, in addition to providing a riff on the road-hockey revolution Hull's slapshot inspired in the 1960s, helped us track down vintage photographs of Hull as a junior star in Niagara. Thanks also to the *Standard*'s Denis Cahill, for hauling boxes of ancient hockey negatives out of storage, and managing editor Doug Firby, for letting us sort through the newspaper's treasure trove of old pictures.

I also wish to thank Peter Goddard for his sleuthing efforts in the *Toronto Star*'s picture library, and Craig Campbell of the Hockey Hall Of Fame for furnishing more than half of the images which appear in this book.

Finally, to my beautiful and understanding wife, Liza, who was nearly as angry as I was when the Leafs let Steve "Stumpy" Thomas sign with Chicago during the off-season.

Grateful acknowledgment is made to the following for use of photographs: the Hockey Hall of Fame (photos on jacket and pages ii, vi–vii, viii, 8, 9, 10, 12, 20, 23, 24, 28, 33, 48, 50, 55, 57, 62, 64, 67, 72–73, 80, 81, 87, 92, 97, 100, 103 (bottom left), 104, 109, 110 (both), 119; the *Toronto Star* library (photos on pages 3, 5, 30–31, 44, 46–47, 52, 58, 60, 68, 71, 76, 103 (top, bottom right)); *St. Catharines Standard* (pages 15, 16–17, 36, 40–41, 43); Craig MacInnis (page 84); and Bill Douglas (page 88).

Grateful acknowledgment is made to reprint "Hay? Hull has it . . . and makes it," by Frank Orr, *Toronto Star*, July 20, 1968.

*Pause that refreshes: Hull takes
a drink while wearing special
headgear to protect his jaw.*

Also Available in the Remembering Series

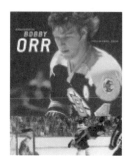

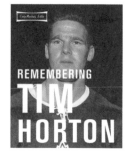

**REMEMBERING
THE ROCKET**

ISBN 0-7737-31288
$22.95 CDN
$14.95 US

**REMEMBERING
BOBBY ORR**

ISBN 0-7737-31962
$22.95 CDN
$19.95 US

**REMEMBERING
TIM HORTON**

ISBN 0-7737-3256-X
$22.95 CDN
$15.95 US

www.stoddartpub.com